I0165772

A
Treasure Trove
of Opportunity

How to
Write & Sell
Articles for
Children's Magazines

Melissa Abramovitz

Copyright © 2012 Melissa Abramovitz
ISBN-13: 978-0-9831499-1-0

Cover image © Sean Gladwell - Fotolia.com

All rights reserved. This book may not be reproduced in whole or in part in any
form, or by any means, without express written permission from the publisher.

Published by:
Eve Heidi Bine-Stock
P.O. Box 3346
Omaha, NE 68103
U.S.A.

Praise for Treasure Trove

1. "Where was this book when I first started writing? After years of pecking for information on magazine writing, it's finally condensed in this concise book. Even as a seasoned writer, I gained additional insight that I'm going to put to use immediately. Melissa does an excellent job of covering everything a new magazine writer needs to know including how to generate ideas, effectively researching, how to query, and what to do when the contract arrives. A must have for anyone thinking about writing for children's magazines." Monica Harris is the author of 9 books and over 170 magazine articles. She writes from Kalamazoo, Michigan where anything from ticks, garden gnomes, and the waking dead inspires her. www.mharrisbooks.com

2. "Lift the cover of *Treasure Trove of Opportunity* to find gold nuggets of writing advice, silver tips on penning articles, and magical gems to transform the wannabe into a best-selling writer. Brimming with gleaming ideas, proofreading pearls, and shiny trinkets of inspiration, this one of a kind "how to" book is, interestingly enough, a "good read." It fits on your writing desk between well-thumbed copies of Strunk and White's handbook and Zinsser's *On Writing Well*. Sift through its *style*-ish treasures, ponder, compose, polish, sell. Then repeat the process!" Sheila Wood Foard is a writing instructor for the Institute of Children's Literature (ICL). Her short nonfiction and fiction have run in numerous national magazines for children and adult readers. Her books include an award-winning young adult historical novel, *HARVEY GIRL* (Texas Tech Press), and a biography for teens of the Mexican muralist Diego Rivera (Chelsea House).

3. "The author has done her homework, and it shows. Each chapter is chock-full of good advice, drawn and illustrated with examples from her own work and the experience of other writers and editors. From interviewing celebrities to the technicalities of formatting manuscripts—if there's a topic she hasn't covered, I can't

think of it. A worthy addition to even a seasoned writer's bookshelf." Christine Venzon has numerous published children's nonfiction articles and books.

4. "Treasure Trove gives a clear overview of the process of finding, researching, writing, and submitting nonfiction ideas, with detailed tips and helpful examples. The tone is comfortable and friendly, so it's like having a mentor beside you. If you want to write articles for children's magazines, you'll want this book." Chris Eboch is the author of *Advanced Plotting* and over a dozen books for children, including *The Eyes of Pharoah*, a mystery in ancient Egypt, and *The Well of Sacrifice*, a Mayan adventure. www.chriseboch.com

5. "This book is INDEED a treasure trove of information for the writer who wants to sell nonfiction material to magazines. As I read, I either thought "I've been preaching that for years, and now I know I'm right" or "I never thought about that, but she's right." The sections on good grammar and spelling would be especially helpful for the beginning writer." Marilyn D. Anderson has had 26 children's books published as well as many, many nonfiction magazine articles. Her most notable work is *COME HOME BARKLEY*, a chapter book about a lost dog. She is also a writing instructor.

6. "Nonfiction is hot but most new writers (and many published ones!) find it intimidating. Writing in a friendly style that feels like you're having a personal conversation with her, Abramovitz guides writers through the ins and outs of writing winning articles for children and teen magazines. Numerous examples help readers see exactly what Abramovitz is talking about. "Treasure Trove" is a gold mine of information!" Bobi Martin is an author, editor, and writing instructor who has sold numerous nonfiction articles.

7. "This book is a treasure trove chock-full of wise, practical advice for the novice as well as the seasoned writer wishing to venture into writing nonfiction for the children's magazine market!

Abramovitz SHOWS how it's done page after page with a compendium of clear examples that demonstrate both the right way and the wrong way in every step of the process from idea generation to query letter. Sit down with a cup of tea and take notes. You're on your way!" Judy Bradbury (www.judybradbury.com) is the author of the Children's Book Corner series of resource books for teachers, librarians, and parents and the Christopher Counts series of picture books for ages 4-7. Her most recent release is *The Read-Aloud Scaffold: Best Books to Enhance Content Area Curriculum.* Judy writes regularly for *Children's Writer, Library Sparks,* and the annual *Writer's Guide,* teaches children's literature and writing for children, and conducts workshops nationally.

8. "*A Treasure Trove of Opportunity: How to Write and Sell Articles for Children's Magazines* provides aspiring nonfiction authors with all the tips they need to become successful children's writers. In her new book, Ms. Abramovitz shows how to develop ideas into articles, how-tos and activities for children's magazines. More importantly, she also takes the reader from queries through marketing to contracts, and from research through structure to revision. In an easy-to-understand format, she explains how prospective authors can pull their work from the bottom of the slush pile to the top of the heap by narrowing the focus of the topic. She also shows that the adage "write what you know" is not nearly as important as being able to write what you can research well. With her age-specific examples, Ms. Abramovitz has provided the nonfiction world with a valuable tool for authors and their potential editors." Renee Heiss has had hundreds of stories and articles published in children's magazines and several books for children and educators. She is also a writing instructor. www.reneeheiss.com

9. "I have one bookshelf in my office devoted to books on writing that I refer to time and again for craft or inspiration. Melissa Abramovitz's book belongs on that shelf." Veda Boyd Jones is the author of numerous magazine articles, short stories, and 42 books.

She has taught writing on the college level. www.vedaboydjones.com

10. "Wow! I'm betting *How to Write and Sell Articles for Children's Magazines* by Melissa Abramovitz quickly becomes THE "Gotta Have" guide for anyone who wishes to write for the children's magazine markets. Abramovitz covers everything an aspiring children's magazine writer needs (and wants) to know. Her clear examples and spot-on advice from published writers, as well as editors, will surely lead many writers from inspiration to publication in their favorite children's magazines!" Suzanne Lieurance is the author of 23 published books and the forthcoming *Become a Writer: 101 Tips for Building a Successful Freelance Writing Business*. She has also published numerous children's magazine articles and is known as The Working Writer's Coach. www.workingwriterscoach.com

11. *"A Treasure Trove of Opportunity: How to Write and Sell Articles for Children's Magazines"* certainly lives up to its name! A treasure in itself, this book is an A to Z guide on how to start—and sustain—a successful freelance career. By providing one of the most comprehensive books out there on this lesser-known publishing opportunity, author Melissa Abramovitz has done a real service to aspiring writers everywhere!" Rosanne Tolin is the editor of the E-zine *Imagination-Café*.

12. "This comprehensive guide to writing children's nonfiction is driven by the author's own experiences as a prolific freelancer, with many insights and examples from magazine editors and other writers. It welcomes aspiring authors with useful information about the entire process of writing an article for children, giving special attention to research methods and relationships with editors." Kathleen Andersen is associate editor of the *Cricket* magazine group's *BABYBUG* and *LADYBUG* magazines.

Table of Contents

Introduction: **Optimum Opportunities** 11

Chapter 1: **Who, What, When, Why, Where** 15
1.1 Who can write children's magazine nonfiction?, 15
1.2 Why write children's magazine nonfiction?, 19
1.3 What is—and is not—children's magazine nonfiction writing?, 23
1.4 When can you start and continue writing?, 27
1.5 Where can you sell articles?, 31

Chapter 2: **Intriguing Ideas**..37
2.1 Find ideas with your five senses, 37
2.2 Pay attention to media, 43
2.3 Pay attention to places you go, 44
2.4 Ideas from memories and experiences, 45
2.5 Ideas from magazine theme lists, 45
2.6 Focusing an idea and finding an angle, 46

Chapter 3: **Salable Structure** 51
3.1 How-to articles, 51
3.2 Puzzles, 54
3.3 Quizzes, 54
3.4 Sidebars, 56
3.5 Quiz show format, 60
3.6 Nonfiction verse, 62
3.7 Personal experience articles, 64
3.8 Slice-of-life or inspirational articles,65
3.9 Profile and As-told-to articles, 68

Chapter 4: **Quality Queries**.. 71
4.1 Advantages of queries, 71
4.2 Presenting your idea and yourself in a query, 73
4.3 Essential elements of a query letter, 74

4.4 Samples of good query letters, 75
4.5 Additional enclosures: resumés and clips, 78
4.6 Query letter no-no's, 80
4.7 Really bad query letters, 82

Chapter 5: **Reliable Research** 87
5.1 Reliable—and not-so-reliable—sources, 87
5.2 Bias in resources, 90
5.3 Timeliness of sources, 91
5.4 Nailing those interviews, 92
5.5 Other research sources, 99
5.6 How much is enough?, 99
5.7 Research notes and organization, 102
5.8 Outlines, 103

Chapter 6: **About Age-Appropriateness**.................................105
6.1 Childrens' interests, 105
6.2 Dumbing down is a no-no, 106
6.3 Age-appropriate references points, 112
6.4 Capabilities and interests of specific age groups, 113
6.5 Magazines for mixed age groups, 126
6.6 Checking age-appropriate words and sentence structure, 127

Chapter 7: **Non-boring Nonfiction** 131
7.1 Creative nonfiction, 131
7.2 Show, don't tell, 133
7.3 Active vs. passive voice, 137
7.4 Making nonfiction fun and accessible, 138
7.5 Using quotes effectively, 142
7.6 Examples, analogies, and anecdotes, 145

Chapter 8: **Terrific Titles and Beguiling Beginnings**..........149
8.1 The importance of the title, 149
8.2 Wordplay, alliteration, rhyme, and other terrific titles, 151
8.3 Deck the halls, 154
8.4 What beguiling beginnings are—and are not, 155

8.5 Effective beginnings—questions, provocative statements, you-are-there leads, 158

Chapter 9: **Magnificent Middles** 163
9.1 Flowing merrily along between ideas and subheads, 163
9.2 Varying words and sentence structure, 167
9.3 Sample articles, 168
9.4 An article that sort of breaks the rules, 176

Chapter 10: **Effervescent Endings** 185
10.1 The title ending, 186
10.2 The significance ending, 187
10.3 Advice endings, 189
10.4 Summary endings, 190
10.5 Quotation endings, 191
10.6 Just plain weird endings, 193
10.7 Full circle endings, 195

Chapter 11: **Formatting Finesse and Radical Revision** 199
11.1 Acceptable formats, 199
11.2 After the text, 200
11.3 Letting the manuscript gel, 201
11.4 Revising after the manuscript gels, 203
11.5 Other editing considerations, 206
11.6 Getting editing help, 208

Chapter 12: **Marketing Magic** 213
12.1 Submitting an assigned article, 213
12.2 Submitting on spec—know the magazine, 215
12.3 Submitting the article, 218
12.4 Photos, 219
12.5 Cover letters, 220
12.6 Exclusive submissions, 223
12.7 Keeping records, 225
12.8 After the manuscript is sent, 226

Chapter 13: **Contract Considerations and Relevant Rights**.229
13.1 Legal considerations and contracts, 229
13.2 Avoid getting burned, 230
13.3 Relevant rights, 232
13.4 Copyright laws, 234
13.5 Copyright infringement, 235
13.6 Everyone's favorite topic—taxes, 237
13.7 After the sale, 238

Chapter 14: **Rejection Resilience** 239
14.1 Reacting to rejections, 239
14.2 Types of rejection letters, 241
14.3 Good rejections, 244
14.4 Rejection resilience, 245

Appendix A: **Grammar Gateway**...249
A.1 Parts of speech, 249
A.2 Spelling challenges, 259
A.3 Sentence structure, 263
A.4 Punctuation pointers, 265
A.5 Unbreakable rules, 273

Appendix B: **Referencing References** 275
B.1 Citing books, 275
B.2 Citing magazine articles, 275
B.3 Citing newspaper articles, 276
B.4 Citing Web references, 276
B.5 Citing interviews, 277
B.6 Sample bibliography, 277

About the Author 279

Introduction
Optimum Opportunities

Writing and selling nonfiction magazine articles for children and teenagers can be rewarding and lucrative. Different magazines pay anywhere from about $20 to over $1000, depending on style and length. While most people who write and publish children's magazine nonfiction do not make a living strictly from this type of writing, some do, and for many others the income is substantial enough to be a welcome supplement to income from other kinds of writing, such as magazine fiction, books, and writing for adults. If you have another job and are not a full-time writer, selling children's nonfiction articles can add some vacation money or a house down payment to your budget.

If you are not a published writer, writing nonfiction for children and teens is an accessible and ideal method of breaking into print. It also provides a reliable, ongoing source of assignments and markets for experienced, widely published authors. Children and teen magazine editors are hungry for well-researched, well-written nonfiction, and the chances of selling magazine nonfiction are far greater than those of selling fiction. "We get ten fiction submissions for every nonfiction submission, and we're always looking for nonfiction to fit in with our themes," says *Hopscotch, Boy's Quest,* and *Fun For Kidz* editor Marilyn Edwards. Other editors echo Edwards' statement. "While we publish roughly the same amount of fiction and nonfiction in *Highlights,* we receive substantially more fiction submissions than nonfiction submissions. As a result, nonfiction has a higher chance of being purchased. We are always looking for new nonfiction writers," says *Highlights* senior editor Debra Hess.

Selling nonfiction magazine articles is also far easier than selling nonfiction or fiction books. Book editors cannot purchase as many manuscripts as magazine editors can because books cost so much more to produce and market. Thus, they are even choosier than magazine editors are (not that magazine editors aren't choosy—believe me, they are!). The fact that most magazines are published monthly also gives magazine editors a greater ongoing need for new material. Freelance writer Anne Renaud started out wanting to publish a children's picture book, but after many rejections realized she had a much better chance of selling nonfiction to children's magazines. She began writing magazine articles and soon made her first sale. "I found it less overwhelming to write an article than a book, plus there's a much greater demand for magazine nonfiction than for books. The fact that I could get published kept me from being discouraged, and later on I started selling books too. But I still enjoy writing and selling magazine articles," she says.

Freelance writer Mark Haverstock, who has published over 550 nonfiction magazine articles, calls the need for children's magazine nonfiction "one of the best kept secrets in the trade." At the risk of divulging well-kept secrets and tips for succeeding in this market, I've written this book to provide a comprehensive guide to planning, researching, writing, and marketing magazine nonfiction for children and teens. There are books out there on writing nonfiction in general and on magazine nonfiction in general, but they offer limited insight into the specifics of writing and selling articles for children and teens. This book will give you the specifics you need to get started in a richly fulfilling and financially rewarding full or part-time career.

Many years ago the keynote speaker at a writer's conference I attended talked about the secret to getting published. She said, "The secret to getting published is to write." She then spent half an hour telling the audience that if they made the time and commitment to write every day, they would be well on their way to publication. Even though this speaker was a renowned novelist, and even though I was not a widely published author at that time, I knew she was vastly oversimplifying the facts. Of course you have to write to get published. But you also have to learn about and do far more than just writing.

Being a successful writer requires good research skills and know-how about communicating in an entertaining and age-appropriate manner. You don't have to be an expert on the topic you're writing about, but you must know how and where to get experts' input. You also need to learn about finding and focusing appropriate ideas, writing winning query letters, choosing your markets, following publishers' guidelines, revising and polishing your manuscripts, and running a business. Yes, freelance writing is a business, and in addition to writing well, you also need some business skills. Salesmanship, market research, signing and adhering to legal contracts, and record keeping and bookkeeping are all part of the gig. So are "people skills" that convey your professionalism and competence to editors and people whom you interview for your articles. Just as cooking a good meal requires behind-the-scenes slicing, dicing, spicing, and other preparations that are not readily visible in the end product, writing and marketing a good, publishable article also must begin with an appreciable amount of prep work.

This book covers all these aspects of writing children's articles, using concrete examples and specific instructions. I won't waste your time with vague advice like "be sure to start your article with an engaging hook," or "don't talk down to children." Instead, I will show you how to develop an engaging hook and will offer examples of just what comprises "talking down to."

The tools of the trade I discuss in this book will enable you to snare article assignments and sell articles whether or not you have been published. Some publications require a publishing history before they will make an assignment, but many do not, and there are many opportunities out there for unpublished writers to receive assignments and to write and submit on speculation (known as "on spec") as well. For example, Brad Riddell, associate editor at *Boys' Life* magazine, is willing to consider article proposals based on their merits rather than strictly on a writer's publishing history. "Good writers come from all walks, and many have never been published. That doesn't stop them from having talent or a good idea," he says. [Editor's note: Brad Riddell left Boys' Life while Treasure Trove was being published. His comments and insight, however, are still valuable additions to this book.]

Highlights senior editor Debra Hess also encourages new writers to submit material. "We are open to nurturing new talent, and it is as much a part of my job to locate good writers and work with them as it is to edit material for publication," she states.

I have been writing and selling nonfiction articles, short stories, poems, educational series books, and picture books for children, teens, and adults for twenty-five years. I love writing, particularly writing for children and teens, and hopefully in this book I will convey some of the fun involved, along with the tricks of the trade that I consider important for succeeding in the business. I've also interviewed other children's nonfiction writers and several magazine editors, and have included their experiences and wisdom as well. I am grateful to each of them for taking the time to share their knowledge, and I believe their input has greatly enhanced the quality of the learning experience on which you are about to embark. Welcome to the exciting world of children's nonfiction articles, and enjoy the journey towards success as you explore this Treasure Trove of Opportunity.

Melissa   Abramovitz

Chapter 1
Who, What, When, Why, Where

Successful writers of both fiction and nonfiction learn to incorporate the five W's: who, what, when, why, and where, into their manuscripts, so I thought it would be appropriate to begin this book by discussing these questions as they relate to writing children's nonfiction articles. Who can and should—or should not—write children's nonfiction? Why choose this type of writing? What—and what not—is children's article writing all about? When should you start, and when can you find time to continue writing? Where can you sell your manuscripts?

1.1 Who Can Write Children's Magazine Nonfiction?

You don't need a degree in journalism or creative writing to successfully write and publish articles for children and teens (or adults, for that matter). I have a degree in psychology and have always loved to write, and I decided to become a professional writer to allow me to be a stay-at-home mom when my children were small. Some children's writers are former or current teachers who like to write and who have insight into what kids like to read about. Writer Suzanne Lieurance, who also teaches writing and is the founder and director of the National Writing for Children Center, is a former classroom teacher who says she started writing children's nonfiction because "I have always enjoyed taking subjects that are often rather complicated and writing about them in ways that kids can easily understand."

Writer Jan Fields, who also teaches writing and edits several excellent Web-based writer forums like Children's Writer E-

News, started out as a staff newspaper reporter, but switched to freelancing for children because "I liked the freedom and the fact that the per article pay was better."

Christine Venzon wrote textbooks before she started freelancing with children's magazine nonfiction. "I'd been writing high school and junior high textbooks for about 10 years, so I had this wealth of information stored up from all the research I'd done. When my biggest client closed the office I worked with, I found out there were other people willing to pay for it. I also knew what issues educators are most concerned about teaching kids," she says.

Other writers of children's articles are scientists, law enforcement personnel, business people, medical professionals, and a vast array of other professions. You don't necessarily need a college degree of any type to become a professional writer, though you do need to possess a competent mastery of language and grammar so you can communicate effectively. You also must have the know-how to understand complex topics and to explain these topics simply and accurately. For instance, I write a great deal on health and medical topics, and often must read articles in medical journals and medical textbooks, as well as consulting more consumer-friendly sources in my research. Though I don't pretend to understand much of the technical jargon about gene polymorphisms and excitatory neurotransmitters and the chemical structure of certain drugs, I am able to comprehend enough to make the basic concepts accessible to my readers. My strong background in physiological psychology has certainly helped me in this regard.

You also don't have to be an expert on the topics you write about, as long as you are willing to do research and consult appropriate experts. Some writing teachers say "write what you know," but this is not necessarily true. Write about what you want to know and are willing to find out about. Some experts in a field do write for children and teens, but many do not and should not because they are not adept at expressing complex subjects in an easily understood manner. Some publications prefer articles written by experts, but most do not have this restriction.

Although anyone, with or without a degree, who wants to, can write, not everyone who writes will sell anything. There is a great deal of worthy competition out there, and writers who fail to do their homework about appropriate topics, markets, vocabulary, research sources, and submission policies will not succeed. That is where this book can help you!

I've heard people say that "anyone can be a published writer." In a sense, this is true. People who cannot sell their manuscripts to a publisher can pay to self-publish in print or electronic forms. Self-publishing primarily applies to books, but people who wish to self-publish essays and articles can also do so in a variety of media. While these individuals certainly have the right to do this, vanity or self-publishing just to see one's name in print gives professional writers a bad name. When people see self-published manuscripts and groan at the poor quality, they often say "getting published is easy, and anyone can be a published writer." (Not all self-published works are bad, but most are.)

People who say that anyone can be a published writer do not realize that professional writers who do this for a living labor long and hard to put together manuscripts that sell. Those who self-publish usually do so because what they write is not good enough to sell to a publisher. And by the way, publishers do not consider self-published material to be published works that someone can list on a resumé or in a cover letter. So, technically, anyone can be a published writer, but only those writers who take the time to learn what they need to know about writing and marketing will sell anything.

To be a successful writer you must also be willing to present yourself and your work in a professional manner. You don't have to dress up to sit at your computer and write, but you do have to regard your writing as a serious business. You must meet your deadlines and approach editors and people you interview in person, by phone, or by email professionally and courteously. You wouldn't hire an accountant who treats you disrespectfully or who fails to complete your taxes on time, nor would you pay a plumber who never shows up for a job or who leaves your house a mess. So why would an editor hire a writer who does sloppy work or who misses deadlines?

There are also several other requirements concerning who can and should be a professional writer. You should love to write, have high standards of excellence, find it rewarding to see your work in print, be willing to persevere through rejections (they happen to every writer), and be willing to accept constructive criticism from editors and revise your work if necessary. If you can't stand the thought of sitting and researching and writing and revising and marketing, a career in writing isn't for you. But if you love what you do, it will shine through in your manuscripts. It will also make it easier to muscle through the frustrations of rejection and the tedium of necessary tasks like documenting research sources and revising and polishing articles.

No matter how proficient a writer you are, revising and polishing are a must. Some writers tend to fall in love with their words and resent anyone, including editors, suggesting that they change anything, but in order to succeed as a freelancer, you must be willing to look at your work critically and recognize that every word or sentence can, and often should, be changed and improved.

Another important thing to think about is that someone who writes for children and teens should like and understand kids (okay, no one really understands teens, but it is possible to empathize with them). I've read in other books about writing that you don't have to like children to successfully write for them. I respectfully disagree. If you think kids are insufferable monsters, you will be hard-pressed not to write in a condescending or hostile manner. To write well for children and teens, you should respect them and be capable of feeling and understanding their wondrous curiosity about the world. You must also be around kids enough to know their interests and capabilities. And sometimes you may even have to interview them. I really don't think that someone who can't stand kids would have the know-how and tact to do all these things.

Which brings me to my last "who" point: there are people besides those who don't like kids who should not write for them. If you're thinking about writing articles for young people to get rich fast, forget it. You're much more likely to win the lottery. Good writers don't write for the money; few get rich. They write because they love to write and take pride in earning their living, or supplementing another career, in this way.

If your intention is to impress youngsters with your vast wisdom or worldly skills, either alter your goals or find another outlet for your talents. The goal of writing children's nonfiction should be to make learning fun, entertaining, and interesting—not to lecture, overwhelm, or impress.

1.2 Why Write Children's Magazine Nonfiction?

The "who" of writing children's magazine nonfiction ties in closely with the "why." Different writers who choose this niche have different reasons for doing so, but most agree on several factors. Most say that one good reason to do this type of writing is that the topics about which you can write are virtually limitless. Kids are curious about everything around them and outside their world, from nature to hard science to careers to biographies.

They and magazine editors love seeing a unique angle on everyday and not-so-everyday subjects, and you as a writer can satisfy your own curiosity and learn a great deal as well. I've learned some fascinating things about animal sleep habits, FBI techniques for catching cybercriminals, dog heroes, teens who help their communities, fitness, diseases, and much, much more in my years of researching and writing kids' nonfiction.

Jan Fields aptly expresses this perk of writing kids' nonfiction when she says, "The most rewarding thing about the children's market to me is the boundless curiosity of the elementary school child. Really, there is almost nothing that doesn't interest them if you just write it well. And I really relate to that kind of curiosity about things. So with that children's market, I can satisfy my curiosity—do tons of research—knowing in the end I'll be able to write and sell an article because kids are just so open in their interests."

Well-known writer Fiona Bayrock, who mostly writes magazine articles and books on quirky science topics, also finds that writing for kids and learning at the same time is a great reason to do this type of work. "I write nonfiction because the world and how its content fit and work together fascinate me and I want to share that with others. I write for kids because I like the fun and freedom I have playing with language and humor in ways adult writing doesn't allow," she says.

Not only is writing children's nonfiction fun and personally enlightening, but another great reason to do it is that it teaches a writer to express him or herself simply, briefly, and clearly. The stringent words limits on children's articles mean that you literally have to make every word count. There is no room for flowery fluff or distracting diversions. You learn to convey a fact or idea in the fewest possible words, while also insuring that these words are understandable and unambiguous. Editors call this "tight" writing.

The skills I've mastered in writing for children have been largely responsible for my ability to also write clearly for adults, without talking down to anyone. I used to write a monthly health column for a local lifestyle magazine in the town where I lived at the time, and many times, adults who read the column thanked me for communicating complex topics simply and understandably. I remember being thrilled when one woman called to tell me that my article on high blood pressure was the first one she had ever read that helped her truly understand what was causing her high blood pressure and how the treatments she was receiving were helping to make her better.

Not that I consider writing for children to be "prep work" for writing for adults! On the contrary, writing for children is a worthy goal in and of itself. But for writers like me who also choose to write for adults, developing the skills of simply communicating complex concepts when writing for children can translate into improved clarity in the other types of writing I do.

Many children's writers find the fact that they are contributing to the education of young people, and perhaps making a difference in kids' lives, to be another good reason for writing children's nonfiction. As Fiona Bayrock states, "It's exciting to think that a child's first exposure to a topic might be something I write. By bringing stories to children about the incredible planet they live on, I like to think I'm contributing to their capacity to care for it. That's hugely rewarding to me. I also hope my asking lots of questions and sharing my wonder about what are often simple everyday things will help kids keep their sense of wonder and curiosity into adulthood."

Many teachers enter that profession because they find it satisfying to help educate kids, and many say that knowing that they helped spark a love of learning in their students makes them feel like they've done something to make the world a better place. Nonfiction writers are a lot like teachers in this respect. Your article on medical discoveries or teen entrepreneurs or endangered animals has the potential to inspire young people to learn more about the subject or even to pursue a career in medicine or business or animal conservation. It also has the potential to show them that reading is a fun and fascinating pastime—perhaps even more fun than playing video games! When kids tell me that they loved my article or when they write a letter to the publication in which it appeared saying that they loved it, I am delighted not only because I take pride in doing a good job, but also because I feel like I have made a tiny positive difference in the world.

Making a difference and feeding childrens' curiosity can intersect with another important reason why writing kids' nonfiction is a compelling option: this type of writing provides the best opportunities for publication (as discussed in the Introduction). Mark Haverstock, for example, says that the vast need for children's articles, plus "the rewards of seeing my work in print and hopefully satisfying a curious young mind" are good reasons why he chooses to write juvenile nonfiction. Keep in mind, however, that even with the many opportunities out there, the key to making sales is to make your material stand out from the competition in a good way. There are many good writers, and the competition to get published is fierce. Tough economic times have also forced many magazines to cut back on the number of freelance articles they purchase. You can gain a competitive edge by honing your writing skills and by understanding what writing good children's nonfiction is all about.

1.3 What is—And Is Not—Children's Magazine Nonfiction Writing?

Writing children's magazine nonfiction is, and is not, many things. First, here are a few things this type of writing is not. A common myth is that writing for children is easy. Twenty-five years of writing and publishing nonfiction for children, teens, and adults have taught me that writing for children and teens is far more difficult than writing for adults is. When you write for kids, you have to think about whether every word and idea is age-appropriate and understandable. It's also much more difficult to convey ideas in the short space allowed for most children's articles.

When you look at a published article that appears to be something that took five minutes to write, rest assured that this is not the case. The easier it looks, the harder it is to achieve. For me, the most difficult articles and books I write are the ones with the 150-200 word limits, written for preschoolers or kindergartners. Every single word must count. Every single word must be age-appropriate. Deciding what to include and what to leave out after doing research is even more challenging.

It's kind of like watching an Olympic gymnast or figure skater. Their seemingly effortless spins and jumps and flips only look effortless because they've put hundreds of hours into perfecting their technique and artistry, and the more hours they have put in, the more effortless the end product appears. Writing a children's article may not take hundreds of hours of practice and preparation, but those well-chosen, well-put-together words are the end product of much planning, research, and execution. So don't be fooled into thinking that writing for kids—even very young kids—is easy.

Another common myth is that nonfiction in general is boring and uncreative. I've heard people say, "All you have to do to write nonfiction is to spit out some facts, like a journalist or reporter or textbook writer does." Nothing could be further from the truth. First of all, many journalists and reporters do not just spit out facts. They spend time crafting well-thought-out reports that flow and convey information in an understandable fashion. Some of them even write in an entertaining and creative manner when it's appropriate. But often, when they are putting together a headline story for a newspaper, the subject matter or the need to fit certain facts into a small space make it inappropriate or impossible to be entertaining or creative. Ditto for most text-books. The goal of most newspaper articles and textbooks is to inform readers of the who, what, when, why, and where as succinctly as possible.

But the aim of writing children's magazine articles is different. These stories have a tight focus and do not have to comprehensively cover all the facts. They never consist of just a list of dry facts. Their primary goal is to entertain a child while the child learns, and children's nonfiction writers employ a variety of techniques to achieve this goal. These techniques require just as much creativity as fiction writing does. A good nonfiction writer conveys facts and ideas using vivid language and storytelling methods that invite readers to come along for the ride and to laugh, cry, or say "cool!" Sometimes nonfiction articles can even read like fiction stories. As writer Christine Venzon says, "Writing for kids forces you to be interesting and creative to get their attention and keep it." The difference between nonfiction and fiction is that the nonfiction is true, not that it's boring.

I will go into depth about the techniques that bring nonfiction to life in later chapters, but here is an example of the beginning of a teen article I wrote, titled "The Knockout Punch of Date Rape Drugs," that sounds a lot like a fiction story, but is true:

"Jenna, a college freshman new to the party circuit, was having a great time at the off-campus party. A cool, good-looking guy named Trevor, who all the other girls were after, was paying a lot of attention to her. She thought he might even offer to drive her home.

"How about another drink?" Trevor asked.

"Sure," Jenna replied.

"Be right back with it," Trevor said.

As she sipped the drink Trevor brought over, Jenna chatted happily and was surprised when she started feeling dizzy and drunk. This was only her second beer, and she usually didn't feel this way at all..."

So children's nonfiction is not uncreative or boring, and it certainly isn't easy. I touched on one more thing it isn't in the "who" section—it isn't simply practice for learning to write and sell articles for adults. No one has ever asked me when I'm going to "graduate up" to writing for adults, possibly because I already do this, but many children's writers say they often get asked that question. Like the "easy" and "boring" myths, the idea that writing for children is just a springboard for writing for adults is simply not true. Writing for children and adults are each worthy and independent goals, and each has unique advantages and challenges.

If writing children's nonfiction is not easy, boring, or practice for bigger and better things, then what is it? Like most worthwhile things in life, it is a mixture of rewarding, challenging, and sometimes frustrating. Discovering and shaping ideas; crafting intriguing titles and beginnings, middles, and endings; and finding just the right way of expressing a complex idea to a first-grader can be challenging and even frustrating. Waking up at three o'clock in the morning and wondering whether the word "nutritious" is too advanced for a second-grader, or realizing that I used a passive sentence in an article, can be frustrating (and tiring). Waiting three months to hear whether or not an editor wants to purchase an article stretches the limits of patience. Receiving a rejection notice is disheartening and leads many writers to question their talent and abilities.

The lonely part of being a writer, if this is your full-time profession, can also be frustrating for some people. Freelancers don't have to go to an office outside their homes to work. They do interact with others when contacting editors or interviewing people in person or by phone or email, but much of the research and writing and rewriting and marketing is a lonely process. Many writers, myself included, don't mind the solitary nature of writing. I love working on my own and not having to go further than my home office to work. I don't need to interact with co-workers. But that's me, and not everyone is as happy with a solitary job as I am.

These aspects of the job are all part of what writing is (though not all writers wake up at 3 A.M. and lie awake while mentally revising an article). But writing kids' nonfiction is also personally and financially rewarding, in addition to being challenging or frustrating, and most successful writers find that the rewards outweigh the frustrations.

Fiona Bayrock finds that both the challenges and rewards make her occupation worthwhile and exciting. "To me, writing an article is like solving a big puzzle. Finding that perfect reference, that perfect angle, that perfect description, and fitting it all together in that little word count is oh-so-satisfying," she says.

For Suzanne Lieurance, the most rewarding and challenging parts of writing children's nonfiction are virtually identical: "The most rewarding part of writing nonfiction for kids—helping them understand something and possibly even enjoy learning about it—is also the most challenging aspect of writing children's nonfiction." But Lieurance, like other successful writers, works through the challenges, and in the end, the rewarding aspects of the job keep her coming back for more challenges.

1.4 When Can You Start and Continue Writing?

If the who, why, and what of writing children's articles appeal to you, your next question may be about when to start and how to find the time to continue writing. As far as when to start, there's no time like the present. It can take awhile before you're ready to start submitting manuscripts, and beginning the process of learning about grammar and writing techniques and marketing will bring you that much closer to bringing your dreams to fruition. If you have another job, including doing other types of writing; if you're a full-time parent or homemaker; or if you're retired and have always wanted to write professionally, you can make the time to embark on a new career path while continuing with your present one.

When I first got started as a writer, writing was secondary to my primary role as a full-time mom and homemaker. I felt fortunate that my husband's job provided us with enough income so I didn't have to work outside the home, but I had always loved writing and wanted to do something challenging that would allow me to earn some supplemental income anyway. I decided to hone my writing skills and learn to market my work through a correspondence course at the Institute of Children's Literature, and I did my classwork when my kids were in preschool three mornings a week or after they were asleep at night. I even sold the very first article I submitted to a publisher (don't worry, after that I got more than my share of rejections, and quickly learned that selling articles was not a piece of cake). But I persevered, and made time to do research and writing in between volunteering at my children's schools, attending their concerts and sporting events, running a home, and chauffeuring them to music lessons and sports practices for many years. Instead of wasting time driving back and forth to take them and pick them up from lessons and practices, I sat in the car and wrote while they were busy. Now that my kids are grown, I write full-time, but for all those years when they were growing up, it was a rewarding and satisfying part-time career for me.

Many writers with families or other jobs regularly get up early in the morning to put in a couple of hours of writing time before the rest of the family awakens. Others figure out other ways of making time to write. Mark Haverstock sold hundreds of articles while working full-time as a teacher for many years. He did much of his writing during his summer teaching breaks, but also fit in writing time during the rest of the year while juggling career and family obligations. Anne Renaud works full-time as an administrative assistant and does most of her writing on weekends. She also manages to squeeze in some internet research or manuscript editing during her lunch breaks while she is at work.

My friend Alice started writing for children when she was in her sixties and had to stay home to care for her disabled husband. Writing provided a welcome diversion and some extra income, and she worked around her other responsibilities to make time to do it. Her daughter helped out by caring for Alice's husband while Alice wrote and did errands, and a local caregiver relief program provided respite care to give Alice some time to herself when she could write as well.

Some people have difficulty sticking to a writing schedule, and in such cases it can be helpful to set some concrete, realistic weekly and monthly goals. You could decide, for example, to send out one query letter a week until you get an assignment, or to write one spec article every two weeks. Then, you might commit to doing two or three hours of research or writing or marketing per day to meet an assignment deadline or to complete or try to sell a spec article. You can always modify your goals and time allotment depending on your current situation, but are more likely to stick with a plan if you make the goals concrete, rather than vague (as in "I want to sell a bunch of articles this year").

Some writers find it useful to formulate their goals around dollar amounts. If you hope to earn $1000 a month, $50 per hour, or whatever, from article writing, figure out how many articles you need to sell and how long it takes you to compose query letters and do research, writing, editing, and marketing. This will vary from person to person and from article to article, but it's possible to make some educated guesses after you've experienced the process a few times. Some short articles can be completed in a couple of hours, after the research is done. A personal experience article can also be done pretty quickly. Other manuscripts may take a couple of weeks of intermittent work because arranging and conducting interviews and getting to the library to do research may not happen all at once.

Going back to the example of setting a goal of earning $1000 per month, you would have to sell two $500 articles or ten $100 articles to achieve this goal, and this may require sending out twenty query letters, doing fifteen hours of research, devoting twenty hours to actual writing, etc., depending on the rate of pay at a particular publication and on your personal skills. You can never be sure that a particular query or article will result in a sale, though, and some publications don't pay until the article is published rather than when it is accepted, so I don't find it useful to set hourly or monthly dollar goals. But many writers find that this technique helps motivate them to stick to a writing schedule.

Naturally, completing your research, writing, and everything else in the shortest possible amount of time means a higher hourly rate of pay. But don't be tempted to skimp on any of the necessary steps in the writing process just to bolster your bottom line. I do as much research, writing, rewriting, and marketing as needed to do a complete, accurate, targeted job. If this means that I make less of an hourly profit, so be it. I'm much more concerned about forging ongoing business relationships with editors and with maintaining my standards of excellence than with earning a few extra bucks. Yes, time is money, but to me the loss of pride or reputation that would result from rushing or skimping would be far too costly to consider.

That said, freelance writing is a business, and if you're a dedicated professional, you deserve to be compensated for your time. So don't allow yourself to waste time writing articles that no one will buy, unless you enjoy doing this for fun. Learn what's appropriate and in demand. I will talk about how to determine appropriateness and demand in the "Where" section of this chapter and in Chapters 6 and 12.

Another way of avoiding wasting time is to teach yourself to be careful about writing down the author, title, page number, and other identifying information about a source you consulted at the library or online. Going back to gather this information can be very time-consuming.

It's also important to educate yourself about proper manuscript formatting so you don't have to do everything over again. See Chapter 11 for details on formatting.

Since you are your own boss when you do freelance writing (although you do work as an independent contractor for certain editors who give you assignments), no one will be looking over your shoulder or checking a time clock to see if you put in the three hours of research time you promised yourself you would do on a given day. You are responsible for pushing yourself to do the job and to do it well. That can be very freeing and challenging at the same time.

1.5 Where Can You Sell Articles?

Many writers believe that if they put in the time to come up with a good idea and write a good article, it will sell itself. This is not true. Just as a car manufacturer does market research before trying to sell its products, writers must do the same before trying to sell their ideas or articles.

There are literally hundreds of children's magazines where you can submit your work, ranging from general-interest publications to those that focus on a particular religion, on boys or girls, on hobbies or special interests like ballet or skateboarding, or on specific topics like math or nature or history. The key to selling articles to these publications is finding out what they want and figuring out how to satisfy their needs. The best way to achieve this is to study the publication and to write about things that interest you, while following the writer's guidelines. As Jan Fields puts it, "Look for where your passion intersects their mission."

Writer's market guides can be a writer's best friend in the quest to find out about different publications' needs and wants. The Institute of Children's Literature's *Magazine Markets for Children's Writers* and Writer's Digest's *Children's Writers and Illustrators Market* are excellent resources. The Writer's Digest guide is available in book and online forms. Both the ICL and the Writer's Digest books contain listings and information for other aspects of writing beyond children's magazine nonfiction, but of course you can pick and choose what you want to look up. The ICL guide, for example, includes listings on children's magazine fiction, national and regional parenting magazines, publications written for educators and other adults who work with children, and family-oriented magazines. The Writer's Digest guide lists children's book publishers, agents, art representatives, and illustrator information along with nonfiction and fiction magazine markets. Both guides contain information about writing contests, which can be another lucrative method of earning some cash. A variety of publishers and organizations sponsor writing contests of various types; some require a submission fee, and some do not. Even those that require a fee are often worth entering because the prizes can be substantial. Of course, the competition is also substantial, and there is no guarantee that you will win. I have entered a few children's writers contests and have never won. However, I did win a book contest with an adult novella I wrote, and this led to its publication. So don't rule out writing contests; just be sure you tailor your submissions to the contest requirements to give yourself the best chances of winning.

Once you have a market guide, it will open up a world of publishing opportunities. You will find out what magazines are out there, what editors are looking for, and what their word limits and submission requirements are. Some magazines require a query letter and will not accept unsolicited manuscripts. Others have theme lists and do not accept material outside the stated themes. Still others pre-determine the topics they cover in-house, then hire freelancers to write articles on an assignment basis. For the latter, it would be appropriate to submit a letter detailing your expertise and experience, rather than submitting an idea or manuscript. It's important to study these guidelines and to pay attention to subject matter constraints and age groups addressed by a particular magazine before sending a query letter or manuscript.

If you are interested in submitting to a particular magazine, it is essential to study copies of the publication as part of your market research. You can sometimes find copies in a library, and if not, the market guide listings or the publisher's website will tell you how to request sample copies. This will cost a few dollars, but is well worth the investment, as it will give you insight into the magazine's style and focus beyond what you can gain from reading a market guide listing. Reading a magazine from cover-to-cover will tell you which publications prefer an informal, interactive, conversational approach and which favor a third-person approach that presents facts and anecdotes without directly addressing the reader. Some magazine websites allow viewers to see past issues online, so explore this possibility before purchasing any copies.

It's also essential to consult the magazine's website for updated submissions policies, changing needs, changes in editorial staff members, and detailed guidelines before you submit a query or manuscript. While market guides are updated yearly, things can change after these resources are published. Another good way of keeping up with changes in policies or needs is by subscribing to monthly print or online writer's publications, such as the ICL's *Children's Writer Newsletter*, *Writer's Digest Magazine*, the online Children's Writer ENews, or the online KidMagWriters.com.

Publisher's websites also often contain much more detailed writer's guidelines than the market guides do. The *Highlights for Children* website guidelines, for example, go into detail about the editors' preferences: "We prefer research based on firsthand experience, consultations with experts, or primary sources. Biographies of individuals who have made significant artistic, scientific, or humanitarian contributions are strengthened by the inclusion of formative childhood experiences. We prefer biographies that are rich in quotes and anecdotes and that place the subject in a historical context." Studying these guidelines, along with studying back issues of the magazine, will give you the best insight into what is likely to sell to a particular magazine.

Jan Fields shared an anecdote with me about how carefully studying magazines and writing about something that interested her led to her first article sale. I'm going to share her story here, with the caveat that most of the time, violating submission rules like she did will lead to a rejection. Jan got lucky because her article was perfect for the publication, and her experience illustrates the fact that studying *both* the magazine and the writer's guidelines is the best bet, especially in the current market situation, where the ease of writing and editing manuscripts on a computer has vastly increased the number of writers who compete for publication.

Here is Jan's anecdote: "It was the early 1980's and I'd decided newspaper work wasn't for me. I knew nothing about market guides or the proper way to submit to magazines. So I just went to my mom's house and went through her magazines (she loved magazines and held onto issues forever). I read these magazines cover to cover, jotting down ideas that seemed right for them. I got the address and editor name from the magazine's masthead. Then I decided on what idea seemed most appealing to me. I had jotted down an idea about how to design a three-dimensional stuffed animal from paper patterns (which are flat by definition). Since I loved creating patterns for stuffed toys and dolls, I'd given a lot of thought to how this worked—so I was my own "expert." I wrote that piece for *Teddy Bear and Friends* and they bought it immediately even though I violated so many "rules" of submission that it's actually kind of funny, but it was exactly the kind of thing they liked. And I knew it was because I'd read this magazine intensively."

So what rules of submission did Jan violate? She didn't read the writer's guidelines; asked for writer's guidelines when she sent the submission, showing the editor that she hadn't read them; and did the captions, text on line drawings, and photos wrong. Many editors would not have let these details slide.

Off and Running

Now that you know the basics about the who, what, when, why, and where of children's article writing, in subsequent chapters of this book I will go into detail about the many aspects of querying, doing research, writing, rewriting, and marketing that this chapter touched on. But first, in Chapter 2 I'll talk about something that is the basis for all this other stuff—getting and focusing good article ideas.

Chapter 2
Intriguing Ideas

Many people who want to write magazine articles wonder what to write about. Faced with generating an article idea, they draw a blank. But article ideas are everywhere. You just have to train yourself to notice them.

2.1 Find Ideas with Your Five Senses

Your five senses are bombarded by potential ideas every day, and you can easily learn how to harness and develop these perceptions.

2.1.1 Look

First, look at the many sights around you. If you're indoors, look at your computer. When were the first computers invented? How were they different from modern computers? How about the Internet? What makes the Internet good or potentially dangerous? These ideas are all things that might interest kids.

Look at your furniture. How do furniture designers plan what their products look and feel like? Do people in all parts of the world sleep on similar beds? How are different types of fabrics used in furniture made? There are a variety of article ideas in everything you see around you and often take for granted.

If you're outdoors, look at the trees. I was doing just that earlier today and started wondering why the trees that are the last to lose their leaves in the fall are also the first to get new leaves and flowers in the spring. Answering that question might make a great article! Now notice other things around you. How fast do a bee's wings move, and is it true that physicists say bee flight is aerodynamically impossible? How does a bee make a buzzing sound? Does it have a voice box and tongue like mammals do, or does it make noise with its wings?

One day I was walking my dog, and as I looked around, I wondered about exactly how the world looks to a dog. I remembered learning in my college physiology classes that different animals' eyes contain varying numbers of black and white and color receptors, and thought it would be interesting to explore how an identical scene would appear to a variety of animals. I developed this idea into a children's article titled "A Look at Animal Vision" and sold it to *Sierra* magazine.

Another time I was looking at something really mundane: my pocket calendar. I noticed that there were no holidays listed during the month of August. The calendar had at least one pre-printed holiday listing for every month besides August. I wondered whether or not there actually were any holidays in August, and looked at a bunch of pocket, office, and wall calendars in several stores. None listed any August holidays. Then I consulted some books about holidays. I found out that while it is true that there are no national holidays in the United States in August, other countries celebrate a variety of August holidays, and in the United States there are several unofficial commemorative or awareness "holidays" like Women's Equality Day and National Family Day. So I wrote a children's article, titled "Are There Any Holidays In August?" that discussed the origins and traditions associated with some of the August holidays throughout the world. Magazine publishers are always looking for unique seasonal material, and this turned out to be a winner.

Just a quick note about holiday or seasonal article ideas. Different publications have varying lead times, but most require seasonal material to be submitted many months in advance. So check individual publishers' listings for the lead time, but definitely don't plan on sending an article about the origins of Christmas trees in November.

2.1.2 Listen

Listening, as well as looking, can be a fertile source of ideas. Many of the articles I've published originated with something one of my children said. For example, one day my then-six-year-old son asked, "Mommy, is Grover City named after Grover on Sesame Street?" (We lived in San Luis Obispo, California, and Grover City was a nearby town). I assured my son that Grover City had not been named after furry Grover, and he then asked, "Well, who was it named after?" I told him I didn't know, but that we would find out. We went to the library and found the answer in the California history section. Then I started thinking that most area residents probably had no clue about the origins and meaning of their town names, and about how it would be interesting to do an article about the subject for a local lifestyle and history magazine for which I regularly wrote. I researched the origins and meanings of the over twenty town names in the county and wrote the article. Although I wrote it for adults, after it was published, the editor received a great many requests from teachers in all grade levels who wished to reprint it for use in their classrooms, so it ended up being partly a children's article after all!

Conversations with anyone can lead to article ideas, and so can listening to the sounds around you. What makes different birds sing different melodies? How do loud noises hurt the ears? What makes the wind howl? Listen to the radio and other media as well. One day I heard a radio news story about a dog who saved a two-year-old child from being bitten by a rattlesnake. That got me thinking about other stories I'd heard about dog heroes saving lives in the civilian and military worlds—military dogs that alerted troops to an impending ambush, a dog that dragged her family to safety after they were overcome by carbon monoxide, and a dog that kept nudging his human companion's chest because he smelled cancer cells and knew something was wrong. I decided to write an article about dog heroes, and got to interview some very grateful people about the amazing feats of their canine friends.

2.1.3 Taste, Smell, and Touch

You eat every day, but have you ever considered the fact that the food in your mouth might be the source of an article idea? Why do different foods taste salty or sour or sweet? How does the tongue receive taste signals? What in the food contributes to different taste qualities?

Consider where the food came from. Did you grow the vegetables in your garden? Write an article about what kind of soil is needed or on how and when to plant and care for different vegetables. Do you grow organic produce or buy organic foods at the market? Find an article angle about organic foods that hasn't been done to death. Do you know someone whose health changed for the better after they switched to eating organic foods? Did ancient civilizations know about organic gardening? What is different about organic meats and dairy products and snack foods? What are "natural" foods? Are they always healthier than "unnatural" foods? Your dinner could give you tons of ideas!

Notice how foods smell to you. Why does coffee smell different from a sizzling steak? How do smells get from objects to smell receptors in the nose? How far away from an object can people and different animals detect a smell? What can dogs smell that people can't? How do people train detective dogs to respond to the smell of drugs or bombs or certain people?

In researching an assigned article about food allergies, I discovered that the mother of a child with a severe peanut allergy came up with the idea of using specially trained peanut-sniffing dogs as helper dogs, just like people use helper dogs for assistance with seeing or hearing or doing chores. She enlisted the help of a dog trainer and started a national referral and funding foundation for this purpose. I included a section in my article about how the child's peanut-sniffing dog changed her life, enabling her to go places she previously could not go on the off chance that she might get near peanut fragments and go into anaphylactic shock. This could easily have been expanded into a full-length article about how dog noses benefit humanity.

Contemplating your sense of smell could lead to countless other article ideas. Maybe you encountered the nauseating stench of a dead cat on a walk. What makes dead bodies stink? Pretty gross, but intriguing nonetheless. Why do spoiled foods smell bad? Do the microorganisms that grow in them stink, or is it substances these organisms produce? How do biologists believe our ability to distinguish good from bad smells protects us from harm? Does it prevent us from ingesting dangerous substances?

Touch an ice cube. Think about how it feels. Your sense of touch lets you know that it would be unpleasant to touch the ice cube for very long. But what about people who have a rare disease that doesn't allow them to feel pain? They get into all kinds of trouble by touching things that are too hot or too cold. Why does this happen? What useful purpose does pain serve, much as we all hate the sensation?

Now touch a newspaper. How can thin paper come from a tree? Why does very old paper feel weak and crumbly? Why are many people concerned about the diminishing supply of trees because of mankind's insatiable appetite for paper and other tree-derived substances? Did the newspaper come from recycled paper? Why is recycling important? Many kids are involved in community and household recycling efforts. Some take on the responsibility of insuring that their families sort recyclable and nonrecyclable trash. Others help launch recycling programs in communities that lack these programs. Write about these kids. Find a new angle on another aspect of recycling and write about that. For instance, if I ever find the time, I might do an article on the different types of recycling programs in different communities. I became aware that different cities have varying programs when I moved to a new place a couple of years ago. Most cities require residents and businesses to place recyclable materials in special bins or separate recycling garbage cans for pickup with their regular trash. But here, they do what city officials call "non-voluntary" recycling. Residents do not separate recyclable and nonrecyclable items—they all go in the trash together. Then, workers at the garbage processing plant sort through each and every bag or piece of garbage collected around the city and separate out recyclable items. I, and many other residents, find this puzzling and disgusting. The city claims that it results in a higher percentage of trash finding its way to a recycling facility than "voluntary" recycling does, but I find the yuk factor overwhelming. When people voluntarily sort their recyclables, they keep these items separate from the apple cores, half-eaten burgers, potato peels, and dirty diapers they put in their trash. But with "involuntary" recycling, everything gets lumped together. To me, the thought of recycling and reusing a piece of cardboard that was sitting underneath a diaper is not at all appealing.

So how did we get from the sense of touch to recycling practices? That's what can happen when you train yourself to really notice your surroundings and let your ideas take flight.

2.2 Pay Attention to Media

Now use your eyes another way – read, read, read. Most good writers are avid readers. I get article ideas all the time from reading newspapers, magazines, and books of all kinds. Awhile back I was reading a book about animal behavior and came across the interesting fact that horses and cows can sleep lying down or standing up, but only dream when lying down. I started wondering about other unusual animal sleep habits, did some research, queried an editor at *Boys' Life* magazine, and sold them an article called "Quirky Animal Sleep Habits."

Another article idea I got from reading came from a *U.S. News and World Report* article about an ancient Central American game that sort of resembled modern basketball, except that the losers were sacrificed as a religious offering. Older kids would love this, I thought, and they could learn about an ancient civilization in the process. So I wrote "Really Extreme Hoops."

Did I "steal" this idea? No. Ideas cannot be copyrighted, so "stealing" them is not an issue. Many people write about the same or similar ideas—just look at the number of articles out there on grief, divorce, internet scams, celebrities, etc. The key to selling an article about a topic that's already been covered (and most have, in some way, shape, or form) is to adopt a new angle or focus and to write for a new audience (like children). It is not acceptable to copy or rearrange someone else's article itself; that's called plagiarism, and it's illegal as well as being a stupid thing to do. If you get caught plagiarizing, you can be sued, and of course any editor who finds out will avoid you like the plague. When asked about what things will get a writer on her "never work with this person again" list, *Highlights* editor Debra Hess said, "The only writers on my "do not work" list are those who have plagiarized." Plus, anyone who plagiarizes certainly gets no satisfaction or pride out of their writing, so why do it?

But you can't plagiarize ideas, so no, I didn't steal this or any other idea. When I get an idea from a book or magazine or TV or online source, I use the idea as a starting point. I do my own research, interview my own experts, develop my own angle, and tailor the article for a particular audience.

2.3 Pay Attention to Places You Go

You can use your senses separately or all together to generate article ideas, but the important thing is learning to pay attention wherever you are. Jan Fields shares an anecdote about how she got one of her ideas: "Most of my children's informational non-fiction ideas come when something catches my attention—something I didn't know. For instance, I was in a museum and I saw a display about Matthew Henson and the Peary expedition to the North Pole. Now, I knew about Robert Peary, but I'd never heard of Matt Henson and wanted to know more—especially since the museum presented him as this mythic adventurer sainted figure. I did a ton of research to satisfy my own curiosity."

Canadian writer Anne Renaud, who often writes on Canadian history topics, finds article ideas by looking around at local and regional events and asking herself what kids would want to find out about. "I also pick random topics that I want to know about—how were potato chips invented, how were earmuffs invented, what is the story behind cultural celebrations—and write on those things. It has to be something I find interesting because I'll be spending a lot of time with it," she says.

2.4 Ideas from Memories and Experiences

Article ideas can also come from personal memories and experiences. Did you have a memorable experience while defending your country in a war? Write an article that highlights your experience against an historical backdrop. Did you develop a unique method of training a puppy? If it's truly unique, consider sharing it. Did you live on a farm as a kid? Consider writing about how farms today differ from farms thirty years ago. Did you visit Disneyland when it first opened in the 1950's? How has it changed over the years? How did they run the rides and special effects before computers came along? What about Disneyland hasn't changed?

Other times, article ideas spring from your interests or hobbies. Do you build unique birdhouses? Consider writing an age-appropriate article that shares your skills. Do you know someone who makes and sells sculptures crafted from recyclable materials? Write about this person and their craft if it interests you. Do you collect coins or sports memorabilia? Write about the interesting story behind a valuable coin or baseball card. One of the first articles Mark Haverstock sold was on how to build a universal rocket launcher, based on his own hobby.

2.5 Ideas from Magazine Theme Lists

Another great source of ideas is looking at the theme lists provided by magazines that structure each issue around a specific theme. *Hopscotch, Boys' Quest, Odyssey,* and *FACES* are examples of magazines that only accept theme-related submissions. Theme lists can be found on the magazines' websites, and perusing these lists, especially those that present possible subtopics, can help inspire ideas that will fit a publication's needs. For example, the 2011 theme list for *Odyssey*, a science magazine for kids ages 9-14, includes oil spills, the science of staying healthy, trees, the sun, science heroes, and the search for extraterrestrial life, among other topics. Subtopics such as solar cells, sunspots, and the progress of the ongoing Search for Extraterrestrial Intelligence are presented as well.

When Christine Venzon looks at theme lists, she often looks for themes that she can relate to her background in food and nutrition. "I'm always looking for that angle when I read editorial calendars of magazine themes. That has to be your guide too, because editors are very specific about what they want in each issue," she says.

Fiona Bayrock describes how she got an article idea based on a theme list: "Many years ago, as I was looking for an article idea to fit a magazine's upcoming "frogs" theme, my local TV news reported about non-native bullfrogs invading local ponds and wreaking havoc with ecosystems. What a perfect slice of topic—narrow, very specific, interesting and unusual, and fresh. The editor loved the idea, and I ended up writing several articles for the issue on the broader topic of "frogs as alien species" and "how they're being dealt with."

2.6 Focusing an Idea and Finding an Angle

Whatever sparks an article idea, after you come up with something, jot it down and put it in an idea file for present or future consideration. Sometimes you can use it right away, but other times you may be busy with other things, and don't want to forget it. Your idea file can be a computer file, notebook, or index cards in a tin box or file folder – whatever works for you. Some of the ideas you note will not make it to the research and writing stage for various reasons—the idea may be over-used, inappropriate for children and teens, or just seems uninteresting when you revisit it—but it's still worth writing down.

Sometimes an idea that you discard as being too common or inappropriate will sound a whole lot better if you revisit it with a new angle or focus. The eighteenth century British writer Samuel Johnson once said, "The two most engaging powers of an author are to make new things familiar and familiar things new." So take a fresh look at your over-used idea of writing about how to train a puppy. A new angle, such as how a dog trainer taught a dog to alert its peanut-allergic owner if any peanut pieces were nearby, just might lead to a salable article.

Indeed, a tight focus or fresh angle is the critical element that constitutes the bridge between idea and manuscript. Magazines do not want to see articles about general topics. For instance, writing about bears in general would be far too broad a subject. It would be impossible to cover in a single article, and you would not have room to include any details about interesting subtopics. But a narrowly focused piece on what happens to a bear's body when it hibernates would definitely be a possibility.

Mark Haverstock offers some advice on how to get from a general topic idea to a particular angle or focus: "To zoom in on your angle, put your subject or topic idea figuratively under a microscope. Here are some examples of zooming in on your topic to find an angle: Topic: endangered animals. Still a topic: Saving Florida's endangered animals. Angle: Ten steps Florida residents can take to protect endangered green turtles. Topic: Teen drivers. Still a topic: Teen drivers are accident prone. Angle: Why 16- and 17-year-olds have more accidents than any other age group."

Keep in mind that your initial focus can change as you do your research on a subject. For example, you may start out with a plan to write about how the electronics and special effects on the Disneyland rides have improved since the park opened in the 1950's, but during your research you may discover that focusing on one of the original inventors of the Disney technology makes a more compelling story. Or, you may decide to do one article that focuses on the inventor and another on the technological changes. I did just that: I wrote a profile on a man who developed most of the original Disney technology, and another article on some of the technology itself.

Jan Fields shares how she arrived at a marketable focus for a history article after researching Matthew Henson and the Peary expedition to the North Pole and initially thinking that she would focus on Henson: "I found out he did great adventurous stuff and really not so good stuff—in other words he was human. But I also learned so much interesting information about the whole challenge of reaching the North Pole with the technology available to these men. So after reading books, journals, letters from the period, newspaper articles from the period, and magazine articles from the period, I began to narrow the idea down to the most interesting elements. First, the grueling hardship of that dash to the pole and how much it was really a team effort. Second, a murder mystery tied to the expedition that really has never been completely solved. And third, the whole Peary expedition/Cook scandal. But I kept coming back to just how harsh the trip was. That would have been a revelation to me as a kid. So I wrote about that, along with the team elements and sold the article to *Highlights*."

When you narrow your idea's focus, keep in mind that slightly changing the focus can lead to other articles for different magazines and perhaps for different age groups. Thus, you can maximize your sales based on one idea. For instance, you might consider writing one article for 7-9 year olds about how a therapy dog brightened a child's hospital stay, and another article for teens about how to get a pet certified as a therapy dog and how to volunteer as a therapy dog handler at a hospital or nursing home. Your research on a topic will most likely yield much more information than you can use in a single article, and thinking about other angles in advance can save some time if you collect all the information at once.

When thinking about what angles might be appropriate for certain age groups, ask a teacher or parent if you don't have kids of your own. You can also check online on the Google Directory (www.google.com/dirhp). This will give links to a wide variety of topics, articles, and activities for kids of all ages. You can use it to find out what topics might be of interest and how these topics are approached. Another good resource is the Internet Public Library (IPL) kidspace site (www.ipl.org/div/kidspace). This gives links to numerous websites, books, and articles on every imaginable topic. Not only can it help familiarize you with the interests of kids of different ages, but it can also help you find valuable resources when you get to the research stage of your writing.

When selecting and focusing age-appropriate ideas, remember that different magazines have varying restrictions on subject matter. *Highlights*, for example, prohibits material that involves war, crime, or violence, so don't consider writing an article about cybercriminals for them or sending them a personal experience piece about witnessing the attack on Pearl Harbor. But other magazines may welcome such material if it's done in an age-appropriate manner. I did an article on cybercrime for *Boys' Life* and one on internet predators for *Current Health*, so topics that are taboo at one publication may be okay at another.

The Idea Factory

Not every idea you come up with will develop into a viable article. However, once you tune into the possibilities presented by the world around you and learn to narrow your focus, you will be well on your way towards generating an unending supply of ideas that have the potential to keep you busy writing children's articles   for   many   years   to   come.

Chapter 3
Salable Structure

Once you decide on an article idea and focus, the next step is to determine an appropriate structure, or format, for the article. Most magazine nonfiction is written in a narrative prose format (a narrative simply means the telling of a story), but there are subtypes of this structure, as well as other formats. Subtypes of traditional narrative prose articles include profiles, as-told-to stories, slice-of-life stories, and informational articles.

Editors love to see a variety of structures such as how-to articles, quizzes, puzzles, activities, or verse, as well as narrative prose. "Quizzes are great for kids, but I rarely get them. I'd love to see more. How-to's work well also. Anything interactive—particularly for the Web—is good," says Rosanne Tolin, editor of the online magazine *Imagination Café*.

Some topics dictate the article structure—for instance, if you want to share a craft idea or offer tips on how people can improve their diet, the structure will obviously be a how-to. Other times, an editor will specify the structure he or she wants in an assignment letter. Some articles contain a combination of structures; perhaps a quiz incorporated into a narrative prose format.

3.1 How-To Articles

How-to articles are very popular and in great demand at many publications for kids in all age groups. They can also be very lucrative. "The most I was ever paid for a single article was for a how-to piece," Jan Fields says.

A how-to article informs the reader about how to make or do something, and may or may not require research. If you are recounting your own craft project or recipe, you may not need to do any research, unless you include facts that should be verified by an expert source. For example, if you are writing about how to build a birdhouse and bird feeder, and if you write that putting sugar water in a bird feeder is the best way to attract humming-birds, it would be best to verify this fact with a reliable source, even if you have relevant personal experience.

Mark Haverstock explains how he obtained the expertise to serve as his own expert when writing a how-to article based on a long-time personal hobby: "One of my early *Boys' Life* articles was a how-to on building a universal rocket launcher that could use just about any kind of battery—motorcycle, car, lantern bat-tery, etc. It came from a childhood interest in rocketry and a need. The ones typically sold in hobby shops used wimpy AA cells that would run down quickly. Also, I taught some summer enrichment courses in rocketry to 5th and 6th graders."

The bulk of a how-to-make or build something article can be a bulleted or numbered list of directions, but it's also neces-sary to include at least one introductory paragraph explaining the project, discussing why it's unique or fun, and perhaps some background material about how you first came to try out the pro-ject. Additional anecdotes or practical tips are also an asset. If you're writing about how to build a birdhouse, add an anecdote about how your birdhouse has turned your back yard into a bus-tling aviary or include some tips about where to put the bird-house and what sort of food to put inside. This will make the ar-ticle more interesting and salable.

The important thing about the directions in a how-to is that they must be clear and follow a logical order. Don't leave out steps that may seem obvious to you as an experienced adult. It's a good idea to ask a friend or, better yet, a kid, to read over your directions to let you know whether or not the instructions are complete and easily understood.

Some how-to's require diagrams to illustrate key points, and you don't have to be an artist to make some simple diagrams that an editor can later assign an artist to improve upon if necessary. In fact, a how-to is the only type of article for which you should include any sort of sketches, unless you are a professional artist. Editors do not want to see amateur attempts at illustrations in general.

Besides how-to articles that teach a craft or other type of project, there are other types of how-to's that share self-help or practical tips on a particular issue, as in "How to Improve Your Eating Habits," "How to Smooth Over a Fight With Your Best Friend," or "How to Organize a Student Government Campaign." These types of how-to's generally require input from an expert. If you're not a nutritionist, for instance, you should rely on a certified expert or a reliable medical organization for tips on how to improve eating habits. And even though you as an adult may have some insight into smoothing over a fight with your best friend, it would be best to consult a psychologist for this type of article.

As with a how-to that offers instructions on making or building something, a self-help how-to should not just contain a list of suggestions. It also needs a compelling lead with a clear statement of the problem being addressed, anecdotes if appropriate, and a satisfying ending. You might, for example, begin "How to Improve Your Eating Habits" like this: "Poor eating habits cause three million kids to develop type 2 diabetes each year in the United States. An additional one million end up with osteoporosis because they do not eat enough calcium. Yet it's possible to prevent serious diseases like these if you make some simple changes to your diet. Here are ten tips on how you can eat better and healthier..."

3.2 Puzzles

Puzzle activity articles are different from how-to's in that puzzles contain minimal, if any, directions, and, by definition, puzzles are shorter activities. Most publishers do not even refer to puzzles as articles, but I am including them here because many editors need and want a variety of nonfiction puzzles. Crossword puzzles, word searches, choose-the-correct-picture puzzles, and many other types of puzzles are regularly included in magazines for kids of all ages. While puzzles do not generally pay as well as articles do, some writers specialize in creating these activities and sell a great many to kids' magazines.

Many editors like seeing puzzles and other activities that go along with an article, as well as those that stand alone, and including a puzzle or activity can add to an article's salability. In some cases, an editor will specifically request accompanying puzzles. For instance, an editor asked me to include two puzzle activities with an assigned article on snakes. So I created a word search and a find-the-snake-skeleton activity that included pictures of various animal skeletons. Another time I created a crossword puzzle to go along with a health article. It was fun, and also taught me to admire people who regularly put together crosswords—they're very challenging to create!

3.3 Quizzes

A quiz structure is another form of activity that engages and involves the reader. Sometimes a quiz and its answers comprise the main body of the article. Other times, the quiz is just a part of the article or is included as a sidebar.

Making up quizzes can be fun, and they're very popular with editors and readers. But keep in mind that their purpose is to inform as well as entertain. Make sure the quiz and its answers cover what they are intended to cover, and that each question is carefully thought out to convey a concept in an age-appropriate manner. A quiz should not be too easy or too hard.

Here is a quiz I included in an article on bug bites:

Name That Buzz Word

Try this "Name That Buzz Word" quiz to test your biting-insect IQ:

1. This buzzer nests in the ground and in hollow trees. It stings in self-defense if frightened or angry and can sting many times, since its stinger doesn't fall off. Name that buzz word _____.

2. These swarming, biting insects breed in lakes and rivers and are most active during the day. They are attracted to dark colors and particularly seem to enjoy buzzing around peoples' faces. Name that buzz word _____.

3. Females of this blood-sucking species feed on mammal blood. They breed in stagnant water and most often attack in the early morning and evening. They sometimes carry dangerous diseases such as malaria. Name that buzz word _____.

4. Attracted to perfume and flowery prints, this insect leaves its stinger and venom sac in your skin when it delivers its painful bite. Name that buzz word _____.

ANSWERS: 1. Wasp 2. Black fly 3. Mosquito 4. Bee.

After giving the answers to the quiz, I proceeded to give information on appropriate first-aid for bites and ways to avoid each insect. Drawing the reader into taking the quiz is an effective way of piquing interest in the answers and in whatever else follows in the article.

3.4 Sidebars

Quizzes often appear as article sidebars, and there are also other types of sidebars. Sidebars are not an article type; they are boxed additions to the main article that can contain text, graphics, and sometimes photos. I am including them in this chapter because they are an important part of the structure of many articles. Editors like sidebars because they are easily visible and offer a brief diversion from the main text. Many publications encourage or even require article sidebars.

A sidebar can give further details about something mentioned in the text; offer a bulleted list of relevant facts; present brief trivia or factoids; or touch on a closely related topic that is not discussed in the main part of the article.

In a teen article titled "What Is a Medical Emergency?" I included two sidebars; one a quiz to engage the reader in thinking about real-life situations where they would be required to make critical decisions, and the other a summary bulleted list of what doctors consider to be medical emergencies. The quiz went like this:

Is It an Emergency?

Answer yes or no about whether the following situations are medical emergencies. Be ready to explain your answers.

1. Your sister gets stung by a bee. Her arm swells up and she gasps for breath.

2. You hit your head on a table corner. It hurts and you get a small bump, but you are not dizzy.

3. Your friend starts coughing while eating lunch. She can breathe and talk.

4. You see a woman lying unconscious on the sidewalk.

5. Your dad develops sudden severe chest pains He is conscious.

The answer section gave the correct answer, along with a brief explanation of what should be done (like calling 911). The answers are 1. Yes, this is an emergency. Call 911. 2. No, this is not an emergency. 3. No, this is not an emergency as long as she can breathe and talk. 4. Yes, call 911 and check whether she is breathing and has a pulse. 5. Yes, call 911 unless he regularly gets heartburn. If this is the case and an antacid does not alleviate the pain, call 911.

Here is the summary list sidebar:

Specific Medical Emergencies

Emergency medical experts say that the following are all medical emergencies that require immediate attention:

- Difficulty breathing
- Chest or upper abdominal pain or pressure that is new—and severe—in someone who does not routinely get indigestion
- Fainting
- Bleeding that won't stop, or a cut that is an inch or longer where you can see inside the skin layers
- Coughing up or vomiting blood
- Suicidal or homicidal tendencies
- Choking—when someone is unable to talk or breathe
- Shock, with blood flow to the body reduced by some sort of trauma. Symptoms may include bluish lips or fingernails, confusion, anxiety, dizziness, paleness, profuse sweating, rapid pulse, shallow breathing, weakness, or unconsciousness

- Severe allergic reaction to a medication, food, or bee sting; indicated by severe swelling, hives, or difficulty breathing

- Diabetic insulin shock or diabetic coma in which the person loses consciousness

- Burns that involve a large area, are caused by a chemical, or cause problems with breathing

- Broken bones

- Inability to move or a loss of feeling

- Drowning

- Poisoning

Another type of sidebar can add interest and depth to a piece by touching on a topic that is closely related to the article focus. In an article on food allergies, I included such a sidebar about a girl who had a specially trained peanut-sniffing dog to warn her if there were any nearby peanut fragments. In an article on autism, I did a sidebar giving doctors' and parents' tips on how kids should respond to autistic childrens' behaviors. In a piece on the importance of sleep, I included a sidebar about a few interesting animal sleep habits to illustrate the fact that sleep is important for living creatures other than humans.

Sidebars that present interesting, relevant trivia can also be well-received. In an article titled "Humor Can Heal," I included a sidebar called "It's No Joke," that shared some little-known facts:

It's No Joke

Did you know that...

- Laughing 100 times amounts to the same amount of exercise as riding a stationary bicycle for 15 minutes.

- "Twenty seconds of guffawing gives the heart the same workout as three minutes of hard rowing," says Dr. William Fry.

- You use 13 muscles to smile and 50 to frown. Using those 50 frown muscles leads to wrinkles a lot faster than using the 13 smile muscles does.

- People are 30 times likelier to laugh in a group than when alone.

3.5 Quiz Show Format

Going back to the main types of article structures; on occasion you will see a quiz show or a play as an interesting nonfiction format. This can be a fun way of getting a point across, and you don't have to be a scriptwriter to put one together. I've only done one of these—a TV quiz show—at the request of an editor, and it turned out to be a creative and entertaining method of teaching kids about the concept of cheating. It was called "Let's Play 'Who

Wants to Be a Cheater?'" and it did contain fictional elements, so in that respect it would not have been acceptable for all nonfiction markets. But since the editor specified that it should have a fictional setting, it worked fine in this situation.

I looked up some TV scripts to get an idea of how to structure the article, and here's how it began:

Let's Play 'Who Wants to Be a Cheater?'

Characters (in order of appearance): Narrator; Chit Chat, host of the TV quiz show "Who Wants to Be a Cheater?"; Audience; Joe, age 14, a contestant; Joe's conscience.

Narrator: Welcome to "Who Wants to Be a Cheater?" Watch our contestants figure out how to cheat their way to big money—or give in to their consciences, which won't let them cheat! And now, the host of our show, Chit Chat!

Loud Music. Audience cheers and applauds.

Chit Chat: Welcome! Welcome! Our first contestant is Joe! Are you ready to answer some questions about cheating and can you cheat your way to the top, Joe?

Joe: Oh yeah, I'm ready.

Chit Chat: Your first question is: About how many middle school students in the United States admit to cheating in school?

Joe (grinning): I've studied up on that. About 54 percent of middle school students admit that they cheat.

Chit Chat: Right! Your score is now plus $100!

The talk show continued with other questions and surprising twists introduced by Joe's conscience. I won't share the whole thing here, but it was definitely a unique way of exploring the topic of cheating.

3.6 Nonfiction Verse

Another fun article structure is nonfiction verse. Most writers don't do this or do it well, and editors see so much bad verse that many are hesitant to look at it at all. But if you're good at it and are willing to develop perfect meter and rhyme, nonfiction verse can find a home, particularly in magazines for very young children. I happen to love writing nonfiction in rhyme, and I've written several rhyming nonfiction picture books as well as magazine articles. Here is a verse article I had published in the May (Mother's Day) issue of a magazine for preschoolers:

Moms and Kids

Mother's Day is a special day for sharing,

For thanking Mom for her special love and caring.

As you share this Mother's Day with a mother dear to you,

Let's think about some other moms and children too!

A lamb says Happy Mother's Day to a ewe,

And a joey is a baby kangaroo!

Little puppies cuddle close to mother dog,

But little tadpoles swim away from mother frog!

Ducklings learn to swim with mother duck,

While mother hen teaches baby chicks to say "cluck."

Mother cat and baby kittens say "meow,"

And baby calf says "moo" to mother cow.

A mother seal shows baby pups how to float,

While baby kids romp with their mother goat.

Playful cubs follow close to mother bear.

Little foal trots behind his mother mare.

A cygnet's mother is a graceful swan.

A deer's little one is called a fawn.

All these youngsters join in chorus to say

"We wish our moms a Happy Mother's Day!"

3.7 Personal Experience Articles

As I mentioned earlier, most nonfiction articles are written in narrative prose, rather than in rhyme or quiz show or other unusual formats. Not that these unusual formats are not fun and engaging, but most nonfiction lends itself ideally to informational prose. One popular narrative prose structure is the personal experience article. Kids and teens love reading about an exciting or compelling personal experience, but the operative words are exciting, compelling, age-appropriate, and tightly focused. You may think that your recovery from a bitter divorce will make an inspirational personal experience article, but not for children or teens. If, however, your own parents divorced when you were a child, and you found a unique way of coping with shared custody arrangements, this could very well make a good personal experience piece for the right children's magazine, if handled with sensitivity and without preaching.

Many types of personal experiences can be developed into a good children's article with the right angle. Have you had interesting experiences on the job or while traveling? If you're an archaeologist, kids would love finding out about the latest tools you are using to unearth and analyze the artifacts you find. A fireman's story about how she saved a kitten from a fire would be very well received. Kids would definitely not be interested in reading about the luxurious amenities in the room where you stayed at the Flamingo Hilton in Las Vegas, but they might like hearing about how you helped save Elvis' life when he collapsed in the hotel elevator.

A personal experience article need not involve celebrities or well-known events to be intriguing; everyday events handled with a fresh twist can be equally interesting. If you are a special education teacher who finally succeeded in helping a nonverbal autistic child learn to communicate, share your story and its emotional impact on you and the child in a career magazine for teens. You just may motivate a teen to consider this type of career. If a knee injury derailed your plans to become a professional football player and you came up with an alternate game plan after much emotional turmoil, draw your readers into your story by sharing your pain, disappointment, and healing process. But don't hit the reader over the head with a lesson or moral, and don't exaggerate the facts or include irrelevant or inappropriate details just to achieve an effect. And don't write a personal experience article to vent or complain about something that bothers you. Your writing should not be a therapeutic outlet. Write in a journal or consult a therapist if you need therapy. Your purpose in writing a personal experience article should be to share something interesting or poignant or thought-provoking, not to feel better about yourself.

3.8 The Slice-of-Life or Inspirational Articles

Some personal experience articles overlap another article structure called the slice-of-life or inspirational article, though slice-of-life pieces need not be written in the first person, as a personal experience article is by definition. Slice-of-life or inspirational articles are very popular in religious as well as general interest and specialty magazines that cover topics like health, science, sports, history, or hobbies. Such articles not only share an interesting true story, but also inspire soul-searching and emotion in the reader. When properly written, the life lesson or intended moral unfolds through the story's narrative, rather than being overtly wielded like a sledgehammer. Even religious magazines emphasize that they do not want a "preachy" approach.

If you are writing an inspirational article about how your faith sustained you in a time of crisis, for example, don't tell the reader, "You, too can find strength in the Lord when faced with sickness or the death of a loved one." Instead, show how you felt an overwhelming sense of calm as you read a particular verse in the Bible, and let the reader draw his or her own conclusions about how he or she might benefit from doing the same thing.

Non-religious inspirational stories on universal themes of love, friendship, healing, and death can be equally compelling as long as they too do not set out to teach a lesson. It is also important that inspirational stories for kids be realistic, but not sappy or depressing. It's fine if the story elicits tears, but it must not convey hopelessness. Sometimes achieving a balance between emotionally compelling and non-depressing can be challenging, but it is essential that a children's inspirational article contain a sense of hope, even in tragic circumstances.

By definition, an inspirational story should inspire strong feelings—happiness, relief, compassion, or other emotions—in the reader, and many writers struggle with how to achieve this as well. The key is to not resort to contrived attempts to force the emotion. If you tell a joke and say "This is so funny, you've got to laugh!" the joke will fall flat. If you write "You will certainly cry when you hear Clara's story," or "Clara cried and cried for days until she realized that feeling sorry for herself was not productive," rest assured that the reader will not cry or feel inspired. But if you express Clara's story simply and honestly and let the emotional message emerge from the action, rather than telling the reader what to do, the reader is much more likely to be drawn in and feel something.

One of the most widely discussed methods of engaging a reader and bringing a story to life is "show, don't tell." I explain this at length in Chapter 7, but will give an example of it here as it relates to writing an inspirational article for teens. Here is a description of how sixteen-year-old Clara found a way of coping with her impending death:

"After days of railing against fate, Clara finally made the quantum leap that allowed her to face the future with strength and courage. On the morning of May 16, 2009, she sat in front of her living room window, gazing across the street at the Johnston's front yard. The Johnston's two-year-old son, Mickey, romped joyfully in the grass with a black Labrador retriever puppy. Clara smiled at the sight of the exuberant duo and thought, 'Ah, the carefree abandon of new life! The baby and his puppy only know how happy they feel at this moment. No need for them to agonize over pain and morphine injections and the impending end of everything dear to them, as I am doing.' The words 'at this moment' echoed in Clara's mind, over and over again, and she shuddered as she thought, 'This moment is all any of us really have. No one knows what will happen in five minutes or two weeks or next year. This moment is what we make of it.' So Clara focused on what she wanted to make of this moment in her life. She decided that she wanted to tell her parents and her sister how much she loved them and how grateful she was for their patience and understanding. She said aloud, "Mom, I need to tell you something." And at that moment she felt peace, and knew she could face what lay ahead."

When interviewing someone for a slice-of-life article, be sure to ask open-ended questions that require more than a yes or no answer. Say "Tell me what happened next," or "What details do you remember about the scene?" or "How did this event change your life?" Asking open-ended questions is actually a good idea for any type of interview, as we will talk about in the chapter on research. This technique will give you the details you need to make a story authentic and complete.

3.9 Profile and As-Told-To Articles

A profile article can sometimes overlap with a slice-of-life piece, but the two are not the same thing, since a profile generally covers more than one incident in the subject's life. A profile is also similar to a biography, except that a biography is usually a book about a live or deceased person. The important thing to remember about a magazine profile is that it must have a tight focus or theme, unlike a book biography, which can go into much greater depth about many aspects of an individual's life. For example, rather than trying to squeeze everything that is known about Albert Einstein into a profile piece, an article could focus on how he was not a good student because he was so bored in school.

Profiles need not be about famous people; the individual just has to be interesting or has to have done something noteworthy. If the profile subject is not well known, sometimes the only information you will be able to get about the person will come from an interview with the individual himself or from interviews with his family, friends, or colleagues. For famous people, a personal interview is essential if the person is alive, along with obtaining background information from books, articles, diaries, and letters.

A variation of the profile piece is the as-told-to article. Many magazines that accept profiles also accept as-told-to's. Here, a person who has a great true story to tell, but who lacks the know-how or desire to write about it, tells his story to a writer, who then writes the story in the first person. It's as if the subject of the story is telling the story, but the writer actually puts the piece together, mostly using the subject's own words. The byline on such an article reads "By Jamie Jones, as told to Winifred Writer."

So why not just write up the article as a third-person profile piece? An as-told-to in the first person can be more emotionally compelling and detailed, especially when the subject talks about overcoming obstacles or living through a harrowing event. A profile contains mostly the author's words, enhanced by quotes from the subject, but an as-told-to contains mostly the subject's words, edited and enhanced by the author.

Some writers believe that their role in putting together an as-told-to consists of copying down everything the subject says, typing it up, and turning in the manuscript. This is not at all the case. The story must be coherent and complete, and the subject is unlikely to spout forth a coherent, complete story that flows from point to point. The writer must not only ask pointed questions to keep the subject on track and to insure that important details are not left out, but also must arrange nonconsecutive remarks and fragmentary tidbits into a logical progression. Then the author must edit for clarity. Thus, an as-told-to is not a verbatim transcript of everything the subject said. Editors expect a writer to rephrase sentences as necessary, and the writer must inform the subject of this fact and make sure that the subject is comfortable with it. Unlike with a traditional profile, the writer should show the final draft of an as-told-to article to the subject before submitting it for publication. The subject must be satisfied that her story has been accurately portrayed, even if the wording varies from her narration during the interview.

Salable Structures

When choosing an article structure, keep in mind that formats may be combined or intertwined, so you may end up with an inspirational profile or an informational narrative that contains a quiz or a puzzle. The distinctions are not all-important, but it is necessary to know what type of article you are pitching to an editor so you can mention it in a query or cover letter. It is not necessary to make a special reference to an article type, other than indicating it is nonfiction, if what you are submitting is informational narrative prose, but if you are submitting a how-to or a nonfiction rhyme or profile or quiz, or are including a sidebar with the article, this is important to mention.

Chapter 4
Quality Queries

Once you have an idea and have determined an article's focus and structure, you can take one of several next steps. One option is to research and write the article and submit it on speculation to a publication that accepts unsolicited material. Another option is to research and complete the article, then query an editor about whether or not he would like to see the piece. The third option is to do some preliminary research and to submit a query letter and obtain an assignment before completing the research and writing the article.

4.1 Advantages of Queries

Each of these options has advantages, and in some cases, a particular magazine's policies dictate which alternative should be taken. Some publications only accept completed manuscripts, so querying is not an option. This can be advantageous for an unpublished or inexperienced writer because it allows an editor to judge the manuscript strictly on its merits. I often researched and completed articles and sent them out on spec when I first started out as a freelancer, and most of them sold eventually, sometimes on the first try, sometimes not, because I carefully targeted them to appropriate markets. But these days, I rarely do an article on spec because I find that doing the research and writing when I am sure an editor wants to see the finished product is a more efficient use of my time. Sometimes, though, if I have an idea I think will be perfect for a magazine that does not accept queries, I will submit on spec.

For publications that will accept either queries or completed manuscripts, it may be difficult to decide which route to go. Usually, it is advantageous to send a query because then you will not put in all the research and writing time unless you know an editor wants to see the finished product. But if you are as yet unpublished and are submitting to an editor who is wary of giving an assignment to an unpublished writer, obviously sending the manuscript is the right choice. Studying the publication's editorial policies and preferences is essential for helping you make this type of decision.

Some publications only accept queries, rather than completed manuscripts, and this of course dictates that you must go this route. Some editors specify that they only want to see queries about manuscripts that are already completed, but most will accept a query that is essentially an article proposal, and will then either give an assignment or indicate that they are interested in seeing the completed article on spec. An assignment is preferable, since it guarantees that the editor will purchase the piece (unless the writer really messes it up), but even a willingness to consider the article on spec is a positive indication that the topic will be of interest and that a sale will probably result if the article is well-written.

Another advantage of submitting a query and receiving an assignment is that many experts or other people you want to interview as research sources will not speak with you unless you have an assignment. If you call or email a celebrity athlete's public relations agent or a sports team's public relations department, for example, the agent will want to know what the article is about and for which publication you are writing it before they will arrange an interview. Ditto for many experts such as doctors, scientists, or historians. You could, I suppose, say that you are writing the article for ABC Magazine, even if you do not have an assignment, but that's not a good idea because many agents or experts will ask for an editor's contact information so they can verify your assignment and deadline. There are just too many scam artists and people who say they are writers out there, and agents and PR people have to be careful.

Don't get the impression that all experts will refuse to speak with you unless you have an assignment—some will be glad to do so if you explain that you are a freelance writer doing an article on spec for a children's magazine. Just be up front about it.

4.2 Presenting Your Idea and Yourself in a Query

If you decide to send a query letter either because the publisher requires it or in hopes of receiving an assignment, it's important to remember that the query serves to introduce both you and your idea to the editor. A good query letter makes an editor excited about seeing your article not only because the subject matter and angle sound interesting, but also because the writer demonstrates good writing skills and a professional demeanor in the letter.

Not only will an editor want to be reasonably confident that a ++writer will follow through on an assignment, but the editor also wants a sense that the writer is professional and reliable enough to accept responsibility for completing requested manuscript revisions even after payment is made. An error-free, well-written query letter shows that an author takes pride in his work and pays attention to details. So be sure to correct any typos and spell the editor's name correctly before sending out a query letter. The query letter is a sales pitch about who and what you are, and you must sell your professionalism to snare an assignment.

Sharing details about previously published works and including published clips (copies of published articles) can go a long way towards selling an editor on the fact that you are a reliable professional who can complete a job, but even an unpublished writer can convey competence and good writing skills that lead to an assignment. An editor rejected the first idea Fiona Bayrock queried her about, but liked the query letter so much that she contacted Bayrock to ask for article ideas for an upcoming theme issue, even though Bayrock was as yet unpublished. Bayrock suggested something which the editor liked, and this led to Bayrock's first assignment. Bayrock explains why her first query letter was so well received: "My original query letter was very carefully thought out and written with the hope that it would inspire confidence in the editor and communicate that I could follow through with a quality article even though I had absolutely no writing credits. I guess it worked! I was also lucky... the timing happened to be right. I came along right when the editor needed something specific I was able to provide."

4.3 Essential Elements of a Query Letter

So what exactly constitutes a good, professional query letter? A good query letter is brief, yet detailed enough to convince an editor that he wants to see your manuscript or assign you the article. A good query letter:

- Addresses the editor by name
- Is no longer than one page long
- Leads with a compelling hook
- Briefly summarizes the article's unique focus or angle
- Mentions the article structure, if it is other than a narrative informational format, and indicates spe-

cial methods of presenting content, such as case histories or personal anecdotes

- Mentions planned sidebars
- Mentions a tentative title
- Mentions the availability of photos
- Specifies the intended age group and word count
- Mentions how the article fits into a publication's editorial goals or specific departments
- Lists prospective or already consulted sources
- Lists the writer's qualifications or publishing history—not necessarily all his or her published works, but a few relevant examples
- Includes published clips, if available
- Is typed, single spaced, in 12 point Times New Roman or Arial font on plain white paper or letterhead stationary
- Has no typos or misspellings
- Asks the editor to please reply in an enclosed self-addressed stamped envelope (SASE)
- Includes the writer's contact information, including address, phone number, and email address

4.4 Samples of Good Query Letters

Here is an example of a good query letter to an editor with whom the writer has not previously worked. It contains an intriguing hook; provides enough, but not too much detail about the topic and angle; mentions sources; demonstrates familiarity with the publication; and is polite, professional, and conversational without being too casual or too stiff and formal.

Writer's address
Phone number

Email address

The Date

Editor's Name
Highlights
803 Church Street
Honesdale, PA 18431

Dear Ms. Editorname:

Playing on a basketball team is challenging enough when a player can hear what her coaches and teammates are saying or screaming. But Jenny Jones, a talented 12 year-old athlete in New York City, faces an additional challenge. Jenny has been deaf since birth, and loves playing on a local club team. She, along with her coaches, teammates, and a dedicated sign language interpreter, have teamed up to allow Jenny to fully participate in the sport she loves. Together, they have developed a unique nonverbal communication network that not only allows Jenny to "hear" all the calls and plays, but has also evolved into a potent secret weapon against opposing teams.

I am proposing an 800 word article aimed at children ages 8-12 about how Jenny's perseverance and the help of her caring friends and mentors have benefitted both Jenny and her team. In accordance with *Highlights'* emphasis on using primary research sources, I will interview Jenny, some of her teammates and coaches, and Dr. Dudley Demester, who is a nationally recognized expert on athletes who overcome disabilities. I can provide digital photographs of Jenny and her team.

I also plan to include a 100 word sidebar about two professional athletes who have not allowed disabilities to prevent them from shining in their chosen careers.

I have published numerous children's articles in publications such as *Dig, Hopscotch,* and *Science Weekly*, and have enclosed two clips.

Will you kindly let me know whether or not you are interested in seeing my article, which I have tentatively titled "Now That's Teamwork!"? A SASE is included.

Best regards,
Author signature
Author printed name

Enclosures: 2 clips
           SASE

A query letter to an editor with whom you have previously worked can be a bit more informal than one to an editor who is unfamiliar with you and your work, but still must contain essential elements and reflect professionalism. It need not include references to your publishing history, but should not be so brief that it implies that you are assuming the editor will automatically give you the assignment because she has worked with you before. Writing "I've got a great idea for an article on eagle eyes, and you know from my past work that I do reliable research and follow through, so just send along the contract" is definitely not acceptable.

Here is a query I sent to *Boys' Life* editor Brad Riddell, with whom I had previously worked on several occasions. It's more informal than a query to an unfamiliar editor would be, and I emailed it because that is acceptable for repeat authors at this publication, but I remained professional throughout the letter and of course made sure it was error-free. And I got the assignment.

The Date

Hi Brad,

I have an article idea I thought your readers would enjoy, so I'm writing to see if you're interested. Did you know that bats sleep upside down with their feet stuck to the ceiling of their cave? Or that only half of a dolphin's brain sleeps at a time (with the corresponding eye closed), so the other half of the brain can keep the animal swimming to take breaths of air on the water's surface? Then there is the interesting fact that when horses and cows sleep standing up, they do not dream, but they do dream when they sleep lying down.

There are many quirky and interesting animal sleep behaviors. Some of these behaviors enhance safety or survival, while others are just plain weird. In an article I've tentatively titled "Quirky Animal Sleep Habits," I will explore a few of these habits, based on information obtained from authoritative wildlife organizations, books, and an interview with an animal sleep expert. I believe this would fit well in your "Nature" department and anticipate about 500 words.

Please let me know whether or not you are interested in seeing this article. I've enjoyed working with you in the past, and would welcome the opportunity to do so again.

Best regards,
Melissa Abramovitz
Address
Phone number
Email address

4.5 Additional Enclosures: Resumés and Clips

Some publications ask for additional enclosures along with a query letter. Some require a detailed outline of the article, published clips, or a resumé. An outline lists topics and subtopics that will be covered. See Chapter 5 for a sample outline. Most publishers do not ask for a resumé, but those that do are not looking for a resumé that lists all job experience, like one you would use when job hunting (though in a sense, you *are* job hunting when seeking an assignment). A resumé which you enclose with a query letter should cite education and experience relevant to your writing skills and writing career. If you have a degree or job experience in a specialized field that is relevant to the topic about which you are querying, this should also be mentioned. When listing publishing credits or awards in a resumé, a few representative citations will suffice.

The resumé should be single-spaced and not more than one page long. Here is a sample:

Name, address, phone number, email address

Education:
    1995 MA journalism, University of California, Los Angeles
    1993 BA journalism, Arizona State University

Experience:
    1995 - present, Instructor in Journalism, San Fernando Community College

Relevant Published Works:
    May 2009, "So You Want to Be a Writer," *Career World*
    March 2006, "Adding the Photo to Photojournalism," *The College Journalist*
    January 2005, "Tricks of the Trade," *Writer's Digest Magazine*

If you have published clips that you plan to enclose with your query letter, ideally these clips should represent your writing for the age group and subject area about which you are querying. But this is not always possible, and most editors are happy to see a clip about a completely different subject or written for a different age group if it demonstrates your writing style and shows that you can write well.

Erin R. King, editor of *Current Health Teens* magazine, will not make an article assignment unless the writer has published clips, and she offers some advice on choosing the clips to send with a query letter: "The clips need not be from a big-name magazine, but for my needs, a writer has to show that they know how to interview people, properly employ direct quotes from sources, and include research found in primary sources such as medical journals. If you do provide an editor with published clips, it is important that the clips don't misrepresent you. Your clips should not showcase work that required a lot of editing and fixing on the editor's part in order to achieve their published appearance. Editors will be expecting a manuscript similar in style and accuracy to the clips they have read."

4.6 Query Letter No-No's

Editors receive lots and lots of queries, and they reject most for a variety of reasons. Many queries are inappropriate for the publication, poorly written, uninteresting, or sometimes they duplicate an idea the publisher recently used or plans to use. In the latter case, there is nothing you can do about your timing being off. But you can control the query's appropriateness and quality, and it's important to do your homework and to study a publication before submitting an engaging letter that catches the editor's attention in a good way. Editors are busy people, and if your query fails to intrigue them, or even worse, if it is tacky or offensive, the editor will quickly move on to the next letter.

A poorly written query letter is one of the most common reasons for a rejection. *Imagination Café* editor Rosanne Tolin states, "You'd be surprised by the number of query letters I get with sentence fragments, awkward writing, and misspellings. Right there, this is a turn-off, and I don't easily forget about these less-than-stellar introductions."

Boys' Life editor Brad Riddell says another common mistake writers make in query letters is "Not enough information. A query letter is a way to sell your idea. So do your best to sell. If there's a particular angle that "makes" the story, mention it early in the letter. Don't bury the good stuff in the last paragraph or leave it out entirely. Editors look at a great deal of queries and they'll move on if nothing in the first two or three sentences captures their attention." Keep in mind, though, that the query letter cannot be longer than one page, so don't get too detailed!

Another common mistake Riddell sees is a failure to provide an email address. "I make all my assignments via email. If you snail mail a query letter, be sure to include your email address. If you've never written for a publication, you want to make it as easy as possible for them to give you an initial assignment."

Different editors have different preferences about the type of article a new writer is pitching in a query letter, but many prefer to test the waters with a short piece rather than with a full-length feature article. "If you do a standout job on the small stuff, the publication may start coming to you with feature assignments generated in-house," Riddell explains.

Different editors also have varying preferences about word choices and tone in a query letter, but here's one personal preference to think about if you're querying Riddell at *Boys' Life*: "A great many queries start with the word 'imagine.' It's a lazy way of trying to paint a dramatic picture. Show me that you can be more creative than 'Imagine you are...,'" he says.

Other query faux pas are universally disliked by editors. Some writers use colored paper, send handwritten letters, write letters in sparkly ink, use fancy computer fonts or 20 point font size, enclose family photos, or decorate their envelopes to make their query stand out from the crowd. Unfortunately, these tactics make the letter stand out in a negative way. Editors are looking for serious professionals. So be professional.

Part of being professional is familiarizing yourself with a publication's policies and subject matter. *FACES* editor Elizabeth

Carpentiere says, "One of the most common mistakes I encounter is people not taking the time to find out about our publication before submitting a query. We are a theme-based publication and will only consider queries that relate to an upcoming theme."

4.7 Really Bad Query Letters

I made up a couple of really bad query letters to illustrate some of the many errors writers often make. It may seem unbelievable that someone would actually send in letters like these, but I have it on good authority that editors really do see things similar to this (and worse). See how many no-no's you can spot in this letter:

Editor
FACES
Cobblestone Publeshing
30 Grove Street, Suite C
Peterborough, NH 03458

Yo, Editor,

You're gonna love my article called "Playful Playmates." I saw some really cool dolphins at Sea World and figured I'd write about these intellagent playful creatures so I checked out an article on Wikipedia and wrote about where they live and what they eat and how they play adn how they talk to each other. Your readers will find this piece a sure winner! 3,000 words of pure enjoyment.

I want $2000 payment, so after you send me a contract for this I'll send you the article. But hurry, or someone else will snap it up first! I also have some other great ideas that will knock your socks off. I'll send those to you sometime. My neighbors two kids especially liked the piece I wrote about internet predaters. They told me I'm doing my part to keep children in this world safe.

Get back to me quickly!

Joe Shmoe

Let's go over the myriad of disasters in this letter. First of all, the misspelling of "Publishing" in the header might very well land the letter in the trash. If the editor kept reading, she would surely toss it after seeing "Yo, editor." Always address an editor by name, in a professional and respectful manner.

Even though the letter is probably already in the trash, it's useful to consider the other faux pas. Notice the numerous misspellings and missing commas. Understand that it's never, ever acceptable to tell an editor that she will love your article. That is for her to decide. Never use Wikipedia as a source (more on this in Chapter 5); anyone can post anything on it, and it is unreliable. Of course, an article about how dolphins eat, play, and communicate lacks the narrow focus needed for a magazine article, and if the writer had bothered to consult the writer's guidelines for *FACES*, he would have discovered that this publication only publishes articles about culture, geography, and social studies. It also adheres to a theme list, and the word limit for *FACES* is 800 words.

Finally, the last paragraph is a total train wreck. It is entirely unacceptable to mention compensation, contracts, threats of selling the article elsewhere, or other article ideas in a query letter. And never mention that your neighbor's kids or your mother or anyone else loved your article. The editor doesn't care; of course your mother, especially, is going to say she loved it.

Ending a letter with a polite remark such as "Please let me know whether or not you are interested in seeing my article. A SASE is enclosed for your response" and a civilized conclusion such as "Sincerely" or "Kind Regards" or "Yours Truly" is also in order. And always include your contact information.

I composed the following really bad letter to illustrate how an overly stiff, formal approach can also be a turn-off. Sometimes achieving a balance between conveying respect and professionalism on the one hand and showing an editor that you also know how to write in a fun and entertaining fashion can be challenging, but this letter weighs far too heavily on the formal, boring side:

Dear Sir or Madam:

I shall briefly present my idea for a 1000 word nonfiction article on bat communication in this letter. Please be apprised that I hold a PhD in zoology and have published two other articles on this topic.

Bats communicate by echolocation. I think this would be of interest to children because it represents a form of communication to which most of them have not been exposed.

I find your magazine to be of excellent quality and sincerely hope to have the opportunity to see my name in print in one of your upcoming issues. Enclosed you will find one of my published articles and a self-addressed, stamped envelope for your reply.

Yours truly,
Wrobin Writer

Besides being stiff, formal, and boring, this letter has other flaws. Always address a query letter to a specific editor, not to "Dear Sir or Madam." Find the appropriate editor's name in the writer's guidelines or on the magazine's masthead. Some publications specifically state that all query letters should be addressed to "Submissions Editor," but I still recommend addressing it to a particular editor. If you absolutely must send it to an unnamed submissions editor, write "Dear Editor" or "Dear Submissions Editor," not "Dear Sir or Madam."

The first line of this letter indicates that the writer is not at all excited about her proposed topic, so why should an editor be interested? The pitch for the focus is not detailed enough either, and these details should usually precede any mention of the author's qualifications, unless the qualifications are integral to the article idea. For example, if the writer has spent twenty years studying echolocation, this should be stated right off the bat, in combination with describing the idea itself. A good lead might be "During my twenty years of studying echolocation at the Dallas Center for Bat Research, I discovered that bats, like people, interject their unique personalities into their communication style."

Trying to flatter an editor by mentioning that the quality of the magazine is excellent or that the writer really wants to be published in the magazine is not a good idea either. Of course the writer wants to be published in the magazine, or he wouldn't be sending a query. Show the editor why the article will enhance the publication and will be of interest to the readers rather than engaging in flattery or expressions of how you yourself will benefit.

Quality Queries

Once you get the hang of writing high-quality query letters, you will be amazed at the opportunities these letters open for you. And when you land an assignment, you can then go on to the next phases of the writing process.

Chapter 5
Reliable Research

Once you decide on an article topic or receive an assignment, the all-important research phase begins. The quality of the research you do will help determine the salability and quality of your magazine article. Some articles, such as personal experience pieces, do not require research, but for most nonfiction, editors will not purchase an article unless the author has consulted reliable sources.

The best research sources are primary sources, such as interviews with experts or with the subject of a profile article; journal and newspaper articles; diaries; and letters. Secondary sources, like authoritative books and websites, are also acceptable as long as they are authoritative and reliable. According to *Highlights* editor Debra Hess, "The best research is always primary research, including interviews. After that, we look for books from reputable experts with copyright dates that are recent and Websites from universities and libraries."

5.1 Reliable—and Not-so-reliable—Sources

The Internet is a convenient and accessible place to do research, but it is important to be aware of what constitutes authoritative and reliable versus useless Internet sources. Much of what you see on the Internet is unreliable garbage. Anyone can post anything they want to, whether or not it is true, and regardless of whether or not they know what they are talking about.

In general, official federal government Websites (ending in dot gov or dot mil), state government Websites (ending in dot state's initials), reputable educational institutions (ending in dot edu), reputable research organizations (ending in dot org or dot com), and some nonprofit foundations and organizations (ending in dot org) provide accurate, reliable information. Most dot com Websites are personally or commercially motivated, and many are thus unreliable, but this is not always the case, so it's impossible to generalize based on the Website's URL ending. Some people assume that all dot orgs are nonprofits and are reliable, but this also is not necessarily the case, as many have agendas or questionable legitimacy. So it's important to use common sense or to ask a reputable expert about which Internet sources are acceptable sources of information in a particular field.

For example, in doing a lot of medically-oriented research for my work, I have found that the Mayo Clinic Website, which is a dot com, is a very reliable source with articles written by reputable experts. I know that the Mayo Clinic is a reputable institution, so I often consult the Website, even though it is a dot com. Sometimes even commercial dot coms are fine to use in certain cases, as I have found when writing about new drugs or medical technologies. Sometimes the drug or equipment manufacturer Website has the only available information on the new product. Many reputable newspaper and journal sites are also dot coms, and are perfectly fine to use as sources. The *New York Times* website, for example, is a dot com. The dot coms to avoid are personal Websites, unless they are official Websites for celebrities; blogs; and fan-based sites for popular trends or celebrities. Blogs written by experts can occasionally be valuable sources of information, but they are not acceptable for research purposes, since anyone can post a blog.

Many nonprofit foundations like the American Cancer Society or the National Wildlife Federation are reliable dot orgs, but some dot orgs are merely vehicles for promoting political, fundraising, or social agendas and should be avoided. For instance, if you're researching a topic like depression, you'll find many, many dot orgs that on the surface appear legitimate, but are questionable. I would avoid, for example, The Black Dog Institute dot org or the Vitamin D Council dot org, as they lack reputable medical advisory boards and seem to be promoting certain remedies. I often consult government, library, or university websites or well-known professional organizations like the American Psychiatric Association for lists of legitimate nonprofit foundations where I can seek further information.

One dot org to avoid is Wikipedia. Many writers are tempted to consult Wikipedia because it has articles on a wide variety of topics, but anyone can post anything on the site, and its only potential value is to obtain leads on legitimate sources from the reference lists at the end of the articles. Editors do not consider Wikipedia to be an acceptable source, and if a writer cites it, it makes the whole article look bad. Here are a few editors' comments on the subject:

Brad Riddell: "Don't use Wikipedia. And don't go to Web sites that are essentially fan boards."

Debra Hess: "Wikipedia is unacceptable as a source in itself, but the reference list and bibliography at the end of each article may be useful in finding acceptable sources."

Erin King: "As you might guess, Wikipedia is not an acceptable research source in and of itself. Most homespun blogs are not acceptable research sources. And both of these kinds of sites are not always reliable."

Do you see a pattern here?

Using reliable databases, as well as the standard Internet search engines such as Google, can help make your search for authoritative Websites easier. As Erin King points out, "You may be surprised what research sites and databases you can access with your own local library card. Local college libraries will often have even more resources that the public library does not."

My public library allows card holders to access the library's databases on a home computer by typing in the card number on the library's Website, and I find this very helpful for doing research on any topic.

5.2 Bias in Resources

Whatever sources you use, whether Websites, articles, books, or interviews, be aware of particular organizations' or individuals' biases, especially on controversial topics. An article about an oil spill posted on the Green Party Website will no doubt offer a different perspective and interpretation of facts than an article on the Exxon Mobil Website. That doesn't mean you can't present these viewpoints, if appropriate. In fact, presenting both sides of an issue can be educational for older kids. Just be sure that the opinions you include come from legitimate sources and are not just the rantings and ravings of a lunatic blogger who wants to blow up all offshore oil rigs.

Be aware of any biases or agendas on the part of people you interview as well. For example, if you're interviewing a doctor about his work with asthma patients and find out that he recommends unproven herbal remedies, do not rely on this doctor for an objective opinion on asthma therapy. Most magazine editors would not accept this individual's opinion as legitimate.

Commercial-based books are not acceptable research sources either. In writing about many health topics I have come across many books, written by doctors or others, that are nothing more than advertisements for the author's unproven remedy or therapeutic agenda. Many such books have giveaway titles such as "Dr. Jones' Fail-Proof Diet Cure for Cancer," but some actually sound legitimate. I never use any such books in my research. Instead, it's important to stick with objective sources written by experts who are trying to educate the public about a topic without promoting a product or viewpoint.

Another type of source to avoid is children's books. Many editors specifically state that nonfiction children's books are not acceptable research sources, even though most are well-researched and well-documented. It is still a good idea, however, to look at children's books to see how other writers approach a topic for a particular age group.

5.3 Timeliness of Sources

Another important consideration in selecting research sources is timeliness. For some topics, books or articles or Websites that are a few years old or older are fine. For example, if you're researching an historical event or person, primary sources from the period are advantageous, and often older history books are acceptable unless historians have uncovered new evidence about a particular subject. In that case, newer books would essentially "rewrite" the history, and would be important to cite as references.

For non-history topics, up-to-date-sources are essential. If you're writing about an endangered animal, for instance, you need current statistics that are probably only available through authoritative government, university, or nonprofit groups like the World Wildlife Organization Websites. Even books that are only a couple of years old might have outdated information. Long-believed "facts," as well as statistics, can change at a moment's notice. If you're researching the solar system and use a ten-year-old source, you may be fooled into writing that our solar system has nine planets. A more recent source would tell you that scientists no longer consider Pluto to be a planet.

5.4 Nailing Those Interviews

Interviewing experts is one method of obtaining up-to-date information. Many new writers panic at the thought of having to contact people to interview, but whether you are looking for experts on a topic or for people to write a profile about, snaring an interview is not as difficult as it may seem. In all my years of writing professionally, I have only had two people decline to be interviewed, and their reasons were entirely legitimate (leaving for a sabbatical). Many experts, including prominent doctors, athletes, scientists, historians, and others, are delighted to speak with or do an email interview with a freelance writer, especially a writer who writes for children. Many celebrities are willing as well, though getting access to celebrities may be a bit more difficult.

Most experts are much more receptive to speaking with a writer who has an assignment, but there are exceptions, so it never hurts to ask, even if you are writing an article on spec. But forget about interviewing a celebrity unless you have an assignment. The person's agent or public relations representative will usually confirm your assignment and deadline with an editor before arranging an interview.

Locating agents, PR people, experts, and profile subjects can be very easy when you use the Internet. However, as with any type of Internet research, be careful to use legitimate sources. Don't use a blog or a fan-based celebrity Website to try to find an agent's name and contact information. Use the celebrity's official Website or Google "Angelina Jolie agent." Sometimes an editor who has assigned you a particular article will have agent contact information, and that makes it even easier. If the celebrity is a member of a sports team, contact the team's PR department to request an interview. I haven't interviewed a lot of sports celebrities (or many other celebrities, for that matter), but when I have, the sports team PR people were very helpful. The PR departments of the Miami Heat, Pittsburgh Steelers, Philadelphia Flyers, and several other teams, for example, were very accommodating in setting up telephone interviews for an article I wrote on professional athletes who have chronic illnesses. I've also interviewed several Olympic athletes, and the U.S. Olympic Committee was helpful in tracking down the athletes' contact information.

There are many ways of finding non-celebrity experts to interview. Well-known professional organizations are one good method. I consulted the American Dental Association's Website, for example, when I needed to interview a pediatric dentist for an article on tooth care. I sent their PR department an email with my request, and within a day they got back to me with contact information for one of their member spokespeople, who was glad to speak with me when I called.

Here is how I worded my email in this case:

Dear Ms. Smith:

I am a freelance writer working on an article about tooth care for *Current Health Kids* magazine, a Weekly Reader publication for children ages 9-12. I have several brief questions related to experts' tooth care tips, and would like to interview a pediatric dentist by phone or email. Can you assist me in arranging such an interview with one of your member dentists? My deadline is May 10.

I appreciate any help you can offer.

Sincerely,

Melissa Abramovitz
Phone number
Email address

Simple, polite, and direct. That's all it takes.

Other times I locate an expert by reading journal articles or books on a topic and tracking down the author. This is easy if the author has a university, business, or government affiliation, in which case I go to the appropriate Website and obtain contact information. Even if no affiliation is given, sometimes the individual will have a personal Website or is listed in the people white pages on the Web.

If you want to interview a non-expert, non-celebrity for a profile or to ask about personal experiences relevant to your topic, you can often find names and locations in newspaper articles on the topic, or you can ask PR people at a related organization for a referral. For instance, when I was writing an article about dog heroes that saved family members' lives, I found some names and home towns mentioned in various newspaper articles, and I tracked the people down using the Internet white pages.

When I need to interview children or teens for health articles, I find interview subjects in a variety of ways. I located kids for a food allergy article by contacting the primary nonprofit organization devoted to that topic. The PR department gave me the names and contact information for several teens on their teen advisory board, after the PR people first checked with the kids and their parents. (Be aware that you must obtain the parents' permission before you interview a child or teen by phone, email, or in person). I found the name and hometown of another child in a newspaper article, and telephoned the mother to ask if I could interview the girl. For an article I did on autism, I contacted the PR department at a special school for autistic kids, and they put me in touch with a child, his mother, and his teacher.

5.4.1 Preparing for an Interview

Whomever you will be interviewing, it's important to do your homework before you contact the individual. If you're doing a profile on a well-known person, find out all you can beforehand to help you formulate your angle and appropriate questions. No editor will want to see a rehash of information found in other articles. Look for a unique angle that is appropriate for your audience, and explain the angle and intended audience to the interview subject. If you're interviewing someone who is not well-known, you may not be able to get much personal background information prior to the interview, but it's still important to develop a focus and angle. And if you're interviewing an expert on a particular topic, do your homework and find out about the topic and about the individual's contributions to the field.

Figure out what you need and want to gain from the interview, and formulate specific questions to help you reach this goal. Do you mainly want an expert's opinion about a controversial topic? Do you want his recommendations for a how-to piece? Do you want to know how an entertainer got started in the business? Do you want general information about a person's education and hobbies for a profile? Ask the right questions. Do you need photos? Make a note to yourself to be sure to ask.

Doing your homework will allow you to achieve your objectives and will prevent wasting your own and the interviewee's time. Deviating from your prepared questions a bit if you need clarification or if a slight tangent seems interesting is good—indeed, some of the juiciest anecdotes and unique tidbits may come from such deviations. But for the most part, know what you want and stick to getting that information.

An expert will expect that a writer has done a fair amount of research and has developed a focus before the interview. Calling an archaeologist and saying, "Tell me about archaeology," just won't hack it. Let the person know that you've studied the basics and are serious about enriching your article with her first-hand knowledge. If you're writing about innovative new tools archaeologists use, you might say, "I've read that radio carbon dating techniques are being replaced by newer technologies. Which of these technologies have you used in your research, and how do they work?" If you don't understand an answer, ask for clarification. It won't make you look stupid—just thorough and professional.

Keep your intended audience in mind when formulating your interview questions. If you are writing about an athlete for a teen audience, a good question might be, "Tell me a little bit about your high school basketball experiences" or "What advice would you give high school kids who want to play pro basketball?" Always be sure to tell the interviewee which age group you are writing for. This can help him answer questions in an age-appropriate manner, though this will not necessarily happen, and ultimately it is up to you as the writer to weed out quotes that are not age-appropriate and to paraphrase accordingly.

It's important to pose open-ended questions rather than asking questions that can be answered with a simple "yes" or "no." "Yes" and "no" do not make interesting quotes. Instead of asking "Do bears hibernate?' ask "What happens to bears' metabolism when they hibernate?" or "Why do bears hibernate?"

5.4.2 Interview Logistics

The logistics and personal approach, as well as the quality of interview preparation and questions, are also important. Demonstrating professionalism every step of the way is critical. Be there on time for an in-person interview, and telephone on time for a phone interview. If you're interviewing someone in a different time zone than you are, keep this in mind when scheduling a phone interview. Don't plan to call someone who lives in Oregon at 9 AM your time if you live in New York.

Be courteous and appreciative of the person's time and willingness to share their knowledge with you. They don't have to do it. Keep the interview under an hour in most cases—only extensive profile interviews should last longer on occasion. Most interviews rarely exceed twenty or thirty minutes.

Some interviewees or their agents will ask a writer to email a list of questions in advance, and this can help keep an interview on track because the person will know what to expect. It also allows the individual to think about her answers in advance rather than feeling "on the spot." You can always ask additional questions during the interview if needed, so don't think that submitting questions in advance will strictly limit the content.

Many writers and interviewees prefer to conduct an entire interview by email, and this has several advantages. The interviewee can answer questions at his convenience without feeling pressured. Some writers do not like to do email interviews because they believe it restricts the personal interactions and give-and-take that go on by phone or in-person, but I and many other writers find that this is not necessarily true. You can always email the person back for clarification or additional details after they have sent back their replies. An email interview is actually easier for a writer because all you have to do to get a transcript is to print out the email. You're not stuck scribbling as fast as you can to write down all the answers as the subject is speaking. Some writers use a tape recorder to avoid scribbling, but many people are uncomfortable with this, especially during a phone interview. (By the way, it's illegal to tape record a phone conversation without the person's knowledge.)

Email interviews are especially useful for reaching people who live overseas, where a phone call would be expensive or impossible if your calling plan does not include international calls. I've interviewed scientists in England, Israel, and Australia by email, and have been pleasantly surprised that these prominent individuals were happy to respond to an email from a freelance writer in the USA. I got the peoples' names from articles they wrote, and in one case where the scientist had made a recent discovery about the longest insect in the world and received international attention in the popular media, I knew that he had been bombarded with interview requests. I emailed my questions nonetheless, and was delighted when he responded promptly.

Some people you interview will ask to see your article before you turn it in to your editor, but unless the individual is acting as a professional reviewer, this is not a good idea. Most writing instructors advise writers to never let interview subjects see the article before it's published because you as a writer do not need a backseat driver telling you how to improve or edit your manuscript. When people ask to see the article in advance, I always politely let them know that I can't show it to them, and I assure them that I am a stickler for accuracy and will not misrepresent what they have said. That is usually the end of it. Sometimes, though, an interviewee insists on at least reviewing any direct quotes I plan to use. In these cases, I will send a brief list of quotes and ask them to verify that the quotes are accurate. But I never send the entire article.

Many interviewees also ask for a copy of the published article, and this, of course, is an entirely different matter. I always agree to provide an emailed or photocopied version of the final product after it is published. Rarely, a publisher will provide complimentary copies to interview subjects, but this responsibility usually falls to the writer. I don't usually receive enough copies of the magazine to send out the entire issue, but I do scan the article and send out a copy. I keep careful notes on the person's request for a copy and on their contact information in the notebook where I have a page on each article I write. If an article is appearing in an online magazine, that makes it even easier to forward it if requested.

5.5 Other Research Sources

While interviews, books, journal articles, and reliable Internet sources are often adequate for your research needs, don't overlook other sources that can be invaluable for certain projects. For example, historical societies and museum archives offer a treasure trove of primary source information that is not available elsewhere. When I was researching the origins and meanings of local town names, for example, I found some of the facts I needed in library reference books, but turned to the curator of the local historical museum for the remainder. He was a goldmine of information; he knew a great many details off the top of his head, and for things he didn't know, he helped me locate some unpublished scholarly papers in the museum archives. Public or college library special collections and archives are also fertile grounds for primary sources such as old newspapers, diaries, and letters. If you don't know how and where to find these resources, ask a librarian. They are there to help, and many go out of their way to help a writer.

5.6 How Much Is Enough?

So how do you know when to stop doing research? The number of primary and secondary sources you use depends on the subject matter and article length. Many editors, in addition, require writers to verify each fact with three reliable sources, so this requirement may also come into play. *FACES* editor Elizabeth Carpentiere, for example, says, "It is of extreme importance that all facts be verified by at LEAST three sources (and Wikipedia doesn't count!). Our magazines are used in classrooms extensively, and if errors become an issue, it affects your credibility."

Imagination Café editor Rosanne Tolin is another editor who believes verifying each fact with three reputable sources is vital. "I require this, because I like to see sources outside of the Internet. As we all know, Google doesn't always come up with credible sources. It also shows that the author took the time to really do their research. And my (and their) reputation is on the line. I need to know that these are the FACTS," she says.

In most instances, it would be silly to interview three experts for a very short two-hundred-word article. The limited word count would not allow you to incorporate quotes or facts gleaned from this many people. One interview would certainly be sufficient, but then you would also need additional primary or secondary sources for background information. Some editors specify in an assignment letter the exact number of each type of sources they expect the writer to consult; if not, use your own judgment. If you consult a couple of books and journal articles and reliable Websites and the same information keeps being repeated, it's probably not necessary to seek additional sources.

In the case of a profile piece, sometimes your sole source will be the individual being profiled, but other times it is advantageous to also speak with colleagues or friends or family members for additional information. Again, let the situation and your common sense guide your decisions.

In many cases, you will find conflicting facts or statistics in different sources. For example, when researching a health article, you may find out from the Centers for Disease Control that 5 million people in the United States have a particular disease, but a nonprofit advocacy organization Website and books on the topic may indicate that 10 million people have the disease. In that case, it is best to state the most current statistic, which will usually be that from the CDC, since it is the primary official source for health statistics in the country. But what if a very current journal article or book by a recognized authority lists a different statistic? You can either write something like "Experts estimate that 5-10 million people in the United States have X disease," or you can write "The CDC estimates that 5 million people in the United States have X disease, but other reputable sources such as the Mayo Clinic and the National X Disease Association state that the incidence is closer to 10 million."

The same principle applies to other disputed facts or controversies. If your research indicates that some reputable sources believe that stegosaurus was carnivorous, while others say it was omnivorous, share that information, as in "Paleontologists like John Smith at the New York Museum of Natural History interpret this finding as evidence that stegosaurus was carnivorous, while other experts such as Alice Day at The British Museum believe the same evidence tells us that this dinosaur was omnivorous." Again, if you find conflicting facts or opinions in your research, be sure to discard any input from unreliable or uncredentialed sources.

No matter how many sources you use, be sure to include a complete list with your manuscript when you turn it in. Most magazine editors do fact-checking, and they will want to investigate every source you cite. Many will even contact interviewees to verify the accuracy of quotes. Some editors request photocopies of articles, Web pages, or book pages used as sources, and some publications, such as *Highlights*, prefer that the author include an expert review. "We require a bibliography and expert review. We vet all of our nonfiction through topic-specific experts prior to publication. Nothing makes me happier than a well-written article with copies of source documentation and an expert review," says *Highlights* editor Debra Hess.

5.7 Research Notes and Organization

Take careful notes and fully document sources in your notes when doing any type of research. Write down anything that may be relevant. You certainly will not end up using it all, but it's much better to have too many notes than too few. Going back to find a source later on when you discover you need more information is always time-consuming, and taking complete notes can help you avoid having to do this.

I use 8x11 lined paper to take notes, but index cards work well for some writers. I like paper because after I've made notes from one source on a specific point, I can go back and add new related information from a different source on the same page. This helps me organize my notes for the writing phase. But that's just a personal preference. Index cards can be organized the same way.

Some writers prefer to do everything from note-taking to drafting the article on a computer. Some use a smart phone to email themselves notes from an interview or from library research and back up the files on a flash drive or through a computer backup service. Many also print out copies of these notes so they have non-electronic files. Some use a combination approach. Christine Venzon, for example, copies Internet sources into an electronic file and takes notes in a notebook for print sources.

Figure out what system works best for you. I prefer to do all my note-taking, outlining, and drafting in longhand on paper, and then I type in and edit the article on the computer when I get to that point. I like having a hard copy of everything, and I don't like cluttering up the computer and having to retrieve countless notes and files. But different systems work best for different individuals.

5.8 Outlines

Once you have completed your research and have organized your notes by subtopic, it's useful to prepare an outline. Most editors do not require an outline, but most writers find that preparing one makes the actual writing of the article much easier. The outline provides a structure for getting the main points and subpoints across. Here is a sample outline for an article I did on funny animal group names:

1. General statement about animal group names
   a. Most group names convey something about the animals' behavior, habitat, or appearance
   b. Some origins and reasons for animal group names are unknown
2. Examples and origins of behavior-related group names
   a. Tigers
   b. Crows
   c. Cormorants
3. Examples and origins of habitat-related group names
   a. Penguins
   b. Oysters
   c. Bees
4. Examples and origins of appearance-related group names
   a. Peacock
   b. Porcupine
   c. Lion
5. Examples of group names about which experts have no clue
   a. Goldfish
   b. Jellyfish
   c. Ferret

Once you've completed your outline, the real fun—writing the article—begins. If you wish to review some basic grammar pointers and typical trouble spots before beginning to write, see the Grammar Gateway (Appendix A).

Chapter 6
About Age-Appropriateness

In addition to being grammatically correct, children's articles must also be age-appropriate in subject matter, vocabulary choices, and sentence structure. Although rules about age-appropriateness are not carved in stone and may differ among different publications, this chapter will present some basic guidelines about writing for children in general and some caveats for specific age groups.

6.1 Childrens' Interests

One thing that's important for children's writers is understanding what modern kids are interested in and what activities they are likely to participate in. Children and teens do things today that most adults never imagined doing when they were growing up—modern kids are computer-savvy, many text-message non-stop, and many play lots of video games. But they also participate in sports, just like kids have done for generations, and they love reading about science or history or cultural issues if the writer writes in an engaging fashion. So, while modern kids are different from previous generations in some ways, they are similar in other ways, and writers should take the time to acquaint themselves with these similarities and differences. Talk to teachers, help out at a Sunday School, or just listen and observe kids you see in public if you don't have children or grandchildren of your own. The Google Directory (www.google.com/dirhp) and the Internet Public Library kidspace site (www.ipl.org/div/kidspace)

can also give you some good information about the interests of kids of different ages.

Another way of becoming familiar with kids' interests and with what constitutes age-appropriate writing is to read what's being published for different age groups. Read books and magazines in libraries, bookstores, or request sample copies of magazines from publishers. As you study published articles, pay attention to word choices, sentence structure and length, how authors use examples and anecdotes, and how writers go about explaining facts and ideas in a simple, but not dumbed-down manner. This will give you a jumping-off point from which to develop your own style of putting words and sentences together.

6.2 Dumbing-Down is a No-No

Whatever age group you are writing for, one of the most important rules is to never talk down to your audience. Talking down to is also known as dumbing down or addressing in a condescending manner. Editors report that violating this rule is one of the most common reasons that they reject a manuscript. *Boys' Life* editor Brad Riddell says, "Give young people credit. Often a writer will sound like he or she is reading a bedtime story to a 6-month-old. Children who read need to be challenged more than that. Where necessary, define a difficult word or idea for them, just as a boost."

So exactly what does talking down to mean? It means oversimplifying, lecturing, moralizing, or adopting a know-it-all attitude which states or implies that kids are stupid or that they must pay attention to what you're saying because you are an all-knowing adult and they are only children. *Current Health Teens* editor Erin King calls this "being scoldy." King says, "That tone can sometimes come across even when the words aren't straight out scolding readers." Talking down to can also mean trying to be cutesy, which again implies that kids are inferior. Children and editors can easily spot any type of talking down to, and they will stop reading if they see it.

Writing clearly and simply without dumbing down can be challenging. Lots of books and articles about writing for children and teens warn writers about how important this is, but most never offer examples of what talking down to is and how to not do it. So here are some examples.

If you write "Vegetables are good for you, so be good little boys and girls and eat your vegetables for dinner," you are being both condescending and cutesy (as in all-knowing adult trying to cajole silly children). Contrast that with the following, which makes the same point while subtly acknowledging that children are capable of thinking and are worthy of respect; that their reticence to eat some vegetables may be understandable; and that it is still in their best interest to at least consider known facts:

"Do you automatically push anything green to the side of your dinner plate and say 'eeew' when your parents tell you to eat your vegetables? You're not alone. Doctors say about forty percent of kids report that they hate eating vegetables. But doctors also stress that vegetables provide vitamins and minerals which people need to stay healthy. One research study showed that kids who don't eat vegetables are more likely to be overweight. Another study found that kids who don't eat enough vegetables do not grow like they are supposed to. Kids who don't eat vegetables also get sick more often than they should.

"So even though you may think vegetables don't taste as good as ice cream or cookies or hotdogs do, give them another try. Maybe you don't like green beans, but have you tried broccoli? It's tasty by itself, dipped in low-fat salad dressing, or cooked with cheese. Or try adding corn, lettuce, and tomatoes to a taco. These vegetables add taste and make the taco healthier!"

Teens, as well as younger children, will run screaming from a lecture or dumbed-down article. Tempting as it may be to lecture or be blunt, don't insult teens' intelligence by writing "Teens who get pregnant and have babies totally ruin their lives and destroy their futures. So listen to your parents when they tell you not to have sex before marriage!" Think back to your teen-aged years. Would you have listened if someone said or implied that you were too stupid or inexperienced to make your own decisions? It's much more effective to show teens how something affected their peers, and let them draw their own conclusions, as in the following example:

"Kendra, who gave birth to her son, Brandon, when she was fifteen, dropped out of school to care for her baby. The two of them live in a tiny, roach-infested apartment in Los Angeles. Kendra's parents kicked her out of their home, and the boy who got her pregnant won't speak to her. She subsists on welfare and can't work because she can't afford to pay for childcare. Kendra described how having a baby changed her life: 'When I got pregnant, kids at school called me a slut. I felt lousy too. I was always tired and nauseous, and as I got fatter and fatter, my back hurt and my feet swelled up. Since Brandon was born, I'm even more tired. He screams constantly and I rarely get any sleep. Instead of cheering at football games and going to prom and hanging out with my friends, I'm changing diapers and cleaning up baby puke and wondering how I'm going to pay my rent. It really sucks.'"

I find that thinking about my job as a writer as presenting an opportunity to share and explore what I know and have researched, rather than considering it a method of all-knowing instruction, helps me avoid talking down to and lecturing readers. This also helps add a fun element to my articles when the subject matter allows it—kind of like "we're all in this together, so let's have fun exploring and learning about it!" That does not mean, however, that I actively place myself, as the author, in the manuscript. Unless I'm writing a personal experience piece, I keep myself completely out of it. Editors generally do not like it when an author uses "editorial voice" to put him or herself in the article. But my general enthusiasm and respectful attitude toward the reader come through indirectly.

Experts on a topic, as well as other writers, have to be careful about not lecturing or talking down to kids. Experts who want to write for young people must learn how to talk respectfully on the kids' level. This is difficult for many people who are used to using technical language and being in positions of authority on a daily basis. Consider how an emergency room physician might inform kids about the importance of wearing a helmet when riding a bicycle. A no-no would be "I've been an emergency room specialist for fifteen years, and I've seen more than my share of subdural hematomas and other head injuries that resulted from negligence on the patients' part. Most of these traumas could have been prevented by due diligence in consistently wearing a bicycle helmet. Kids just don't get it that being too lazy to wear a helmet will have dire consequences."

It's much better to skip the lecture and the jargon: "I've been an emergency room doctor for fifteen years, and I've treated many head injuries that did not have to happen. A patient named

Daniel, for example, cracked his skull when he fell off his bike and landed on the sidewalk. He was in the hospital for three weeks and still has trouble remembering things. Taking the time to put on a helmet would have prevented Daniel's injury and spared him pain and brain damage."

While much medical, technical, or scientific jargon is way over the heads of most kids, watering down facts or topics by avoiding all big words is another form of dumbing down. An occasional complex word is fine, and can be a vocabulary builder, as long as it is defined and/or given a pronunciation guide. For example, in a kid's article about multiple sclerosis, the name of the disease has to be mentioned, and including a pronunciation guide and a brief explanation—as in [mul-te-pull skler-o-sis]; multiple means many and sclerosis means scars—makes it palatable.

I've even used some really, really complex words in middle-grade (ages 8-12) articles when needed. I used the word "electroencephalograph" in an article on sleep, but included a pronunciation guide and a breakdown and explanation of each part of the word. In this case, watering down the article by stating "Doctors use a machine to measure brain waves during sleep" would have resulted in a vague explanation, so I chose to use the real name of the machine. This would not have worked, however, for younger children. The word "electroencephalograph" is way too advanced, and younger kids would not even understand the concept that the brain emits invisible waves, so this aspect of sleep would not be appropriate to even mention for younger children.

But an occasional word that is a little more complex than a young child is used to is perfectly fine. It's much better to introduce a new word than to imply or state that kids are too young to understand unfamiliar words. The passage "Birds fly to warmer places in winter. Scientists have a word for this, but you're too young to understand it. So just call it 'travel'" is definitely talking down. Instead, write "Birds travel, or migrate, to warmer places in winter. This kind of travel is different than just flying from one tree to another."

Even when writing for teens, remember that using too many complex words will turn the reader off and send him running for a video game. Keep the number of unfamiliar terms to a minimum. The sentence "Researchers are testing the efficacy of the novel immunosuppressive drug golimumab in diminishing the cytokine-mediated autoimmune assault on myelin in multiple sclerosis" would be overwhelming for teens (and many adults). But it could be reworded as "Researchers are testing a new drug called golimumab to see if it decreases the immune system's attack on myelin (the lining of nerve cell axons)" to make it more palatable. Simpler, when possible, is always preferable to complex.

Although it is important to use language that children and teens can understand and relate to, editors do not like it when writers use slang. Kid slang coming from an adult generally sounds phony and contrived; sort of like the adult is trying desperately to be cool. It's okay to insert an occasional slang word or phrase, such as "duh" or "that's pretty cool!" if they do not seem forced, but don't overdo it or use these terms just for the sake of using them. If you are directly quoting a child who uses slang, that, of course, is another matter, and it's perfectly okay.

Current Health Teens editor Erin King offers this advice on the use of slang: "In general, I'd say that kids and teens—like everyone else—can smell insincerity a mile away. If a sentence or passage sounds forced, it's not going to fly with anyone. It's always best to avoid words you aren't comfortable using, and those for which you don't understand the full meaning and allusions behind. I can't think of a good reason to insert slang terms in an article just for the sake of trying to seem cool because there's an excellent chance the words will have the opposite effect."

Highlights editor Debra Hess points out that using slang is also inappropriate for other reasons as well: "One danger is that it can date a story rather quickly. In some instances, slang can also be an indicator of lazy writing."

6.3 Age-Appropriate Reference Points

Another important aspect of using language that kids can relate to is recognizing that children in general, particularly preschool and elementary school-aged kids, have limited experiences compared to adults, and they will not understand many concepts unless the writer compares these concepts to things with which the child is familiar. For example, telling young children that some dinosaurs were twenty feet tall will probably not allow them to visualize the creatures' height. But writing "A T rex was twenty feet tall—about as tall as a three-story house" or "a T rex was twenty feet tall—about as tall as three tall men standing on each other's shoulders" introduces a familiar frame of reference. In a similar manner, don't just say that a tick is five millimeters long. Write "A tick is smaller than your pinky fingernail." In one article for middle-grade kids, I was discussing how much food a paleontologist estimated a twenty-story tall lizard would have to eat every day to stay alive. I quoted the scientist as saying that the lizard would have to eat the equivalent of a sperm whale each day, and added "That's about 1.5 million fast-food fish sandwiches per day."

Be careful about using vague terms such as "big" or "little" as well. These terms don't say a whole lot, especially to a child, who may not know much about these concepts other than that adults are big and kids are little. Instead of writing "Blue whales are huge," use a concrete example, as in "A blue whale can be as long as a basketball court." Instead of saying that a cargo plane can carry a lot of stuff, say "The C-130 is big enough to carry six helicopters and 270 passengers."

Another effective method of helping kids understand a concept or fact is to challenge the child to perform or imagine a simple action. For example, you could write "A frog makes a sound like you make when you burp" or "Taste some lemon juice and you'll know what sour is when your lips pucker!" In one article where I was explaining the concept of a wormhole (a theoretical construct astrophysicists have developed to explain how someone can take the shortest possible path through space), I invited readers to imagine a balloon analogy: "Picture an oblong balloon. To get from one end to the other you can crawl along the surface or you can bend the balloon in half so the two ends are touching. If you burrow a short hole between the ends, you have created a wormhole."

6.4 Capabilities and Interests of Specific Age Groups

The specific analogies and examples you employ, along with word and sentence structure choices, all depend on the age of the children for whom you are writing. Obviously, preschool-aged children would not understand an abstract concept like a wormhole, so such a topic would not be appropriate to introduce for this age group, even with a concrete example.

6.4.1 Preschoolers

Preschoolers generally understand and are interested in familiar, concrete things around them. Pets, books, crayons, toys, cars, trains, snow, the moon, food, gardens, houses, and people in their lives, as well as places they occasionally visit, hold their attention and interest. They also like learning about everyday activities—taking a bath, sleeping, getting potty-trained, or riding in the car. If you use humor in an article for this age group, the humor must be concrete. Preschoolers do not understand abstract humor or other abstract concepts. The child will probably laugh at a reference to an elephant needing a huge bathtub, but will not understand the irony in comparing a dead fish to a person's personality. They will understand that nice people do not go around hitting others, but will not have a clue if you talk about what falling in love or world peace means.

Vocabulary and sentence structure restrictions for preschoolers aged 2-4 or 5 who cannot read on their own are actually less stringent than restrictions are for early readers ages 5 or 6-8. That's because very young children understand more complex words than they can read. However, this does not mean that you can include lots of advanced, unfamiliar words. A few new words, though, helps them expand their vocabulary. For example, if you're writing about animal babies, use correct names, such as a baby kangaroo being called a joey or a baby hare being called a leveret. But refrain from introducing complex words or concepts they just won't understand, such as the fact that animal babies look like their parents because they inherit a submicroscopic genome.

Most sentences for preschoolers and kindergartners are under six or seven words, but slightly longer sentences, up to eleven or twelve words, are okay because someone is usually reading to the child.

Here is a short article written for preschoolers:

WHY DO YOU SNEEZE?

Achoo! A sneeze can be scary! It can be loud and happen suddenly. But it's usually nothing to worry about.

You sneeze to get rid of things that bother your nose. Tiny hairs in your nose trap dust and other things that get in. But if dust or germs get past these hairs, your nose itches. Nerves in your nose tell your brain something is wrong.

Your brain starts the sneeze. Your eyes close. Air whooshes out of your nose and mouth. Out goes the dust or germs! And out flies snot and mucous. Eeew! So cover your mouth and nose when you sneeze!

6.4.2 Children Ages 5-8

Children aged 5-8 are usually referred to as early or emergent readers. Vocabulary and sentence structure must be very simple; the ideal sentence length is four to ten words. Sentences with ten to twelve words are acceptable if they are broken up into two lines, as in
"The dog ran away
when it saw the girl coming."
Sentences should have one or two straightforward phrases or clauses and not be convoluted. The sentence "Healthy snacks help you grow and feel your best" is fine. But "Healthy snacks, which help you grow, as well as feel your best, are important" is way too convoluted.

As with preschoolers, an occasional new word is acceptable. But with early readers, the word should be simple enough for the child to sound out, as in "video." Exceptions to this rule can pass muster if the topic is one that is very familiar. For instance, many kids in this age group are interested in dinosaurs, and would probably recognize terms like stegosaurus and tyrannosaurus.

Early readers are generally interested in more topics outside their home and family than preschoolers are, but still do not understand abstract concepts. They learn new things about the world in school every day, and are eager to expand upon this knowledge when they read magazine articles. Simple articles about science, nature, planets, geography, holidays, health, culture, sports, and historical events are popular with this age group. Kids this age also like very simple how-to articles about making a craft or following a simple recipe that does not require use of the stove.

Many kids of this age also become involved in family activities like recycling, and they are curious about events such as hurricanes and earthquakes. Simple explanations of these topics are appropriate, but it's important not to terrify these children. An article about how to help a parent put together an emergency kit for disasters would be acceptable, but gory details about the suffering of people whose homes are destroyed in an earthquake are taboo.

Here is an example of a short article I wrote for early readers:

A FUN AND SAFE HALLOWEEN

What are you going to be for Halloween? Are you dressing up as an action figure? A princess? A witch? You'll have more fun if the costume is safe. Eyes holes in a mask must let you see out. Otherwise you might bump into things. Can you breathe with the mask? That's pretty important too! Make sure you can't trip over a long costume. That would not be fun.

Can others see you in the dark? You want drivers and walkers to know you're there. Otherwise, they might bump into you. Ouch! So wear a glow-necklace or carry a glowing treat bag. Carry a flashlight too.

Stick with your parents when trick-or-treating. Getting lost or crossing a busy street would not be a good idea. Only go to houses where the porch light is on. If it's off, the people may not want trick-or-treaters. And never go into anyone's house, even if they say it's okay.

Before you eat any treats, let your parents check them out. Throw away anything that's not in an original wrapper. It might not be safe. When you dig into the wrapped candy, go slow! No need to eat it all at once. Why ruin a fun time with a tummyache?

6.4.3 Fluent Readers Ages 9-12

Children ages 8 or 9-12 are considered fluent or middle-grade readers. They are old enough to understand more advanced concepts than 5-8-year-olds, but are still young enough that scaring them with gory details is not acceptable. But articles on science, health, culture, history, nature, sports, and global issues for middle-graders can be much more in-depth than those for younger kids can be, partly because allowable word counts are significantly higher than for 2-8- year-olds. Middle graders are not ready, however, for articles on teen topics like dating or time management or wearing makeup. They do receive drug awareness and peer pressure education in school, so topics along these lines are acceptable if they are handled simply and in a non-threatening manner. Kids this age can also understand some abstract concepts, and they appreciate wordplay and other forms of abstract humor.

Sentence structure and length must still be simple and short for middle graders. Sentences should be under twenty words and should not have more than two or three short phrases or clauses. Sentences around ten or twelve words are preferable to longer ones. As with younger kids, introducing new words is fine, but using familiar words for the most part is best.

Text in an article must be broken up into sub-headings every few paragraphs. This makes the layout less intimidating and much easier to digest.

Here is an article about animal tails I wrote for this age group:

TELLTALE TAILS

Tails tell tales! Many animals give and get clues about others of their kind by "talking" with their tails. Tails also serve as tools for steering, sailing, balancing, swinging, sweeping, playing tricks, and fighting.

Wags and Warnings

You have probably seen "talking" tails. Dogs and cats often send messages this way. When your dog wags its tail so hard the whole dog wags with it, you get a strong message that your pet is happy to see you. If your dog spots a squirrel, its tail stops wagging and goes up. This tail message says, "I've spotted something interesting, and I'm paying close attention." Oh no! Now you've discovered a chewed-up shoe on your bedroom floor. Your dog seems to know you're upset and tucks its tail between its legs. You have no trouble reading this tail message: "I fear your power. *Please* don't spank me."

Dogs' wild relatives—wolves, foxes, and coyotes—use their tails to communicate greetings, show alertness, and signal fear, just like your dog does.

Cats are great tail-talkers too. Your cat points its tail straight up when greeting you or other family pets. All of a sudden, zip, zoom, the tail crooks, and kitty begins racing upstairs, downstairs, and all around the house. That U-shaped tail is a clue to your pet's playful mood. Is your cat lashing its tail? If so, back off. That whipping tail is a message of irritation and readiness to attack. You may be about to receive a claw swat!

True wild cats—mountain lions, ocelots, tigers, and others—use tail signals similar to their house cat cousins.

Beavers are another animal that talk with their tails. Beavers communicate danger to other beavers by slapping the water with their paddle-shaped tails.

Some birds, including peacocks and male turkeys, fan their colorful tails to advertise that they are looking for a mate. Their tails are like a sign that communicates "Yoo hoo! I'm the most attractive guy around here!"

Nose-Warmer, Parachute...

Tails do much more than talking. They are tools that help animals with a variety of things. Tails make a cozy nose-warmer for some creatures. Wolves, foxes, and squirrels curl up and tuck their noses into the fluffy tail hairs during the winter. Squirrels also use their tails as parachutes when they leap from high tree branches to lower limbs. Their tails fan out and slow the fall.

Many birds also use their tails to go places. The tail helps them balance on a perch or slow down and turn during flight. Hummingbird tails help them hover. Many other animals use their tails for getting around too: fish, whales, otters, muskrats, lizards, and crayfish are just a few. In these cases, a wagging tail serves as a propeller or rudder rather than as a communication device.

Some animals swing by their tails! Fun! The tail coils around a branch in a tight grip. Tails used for gripping and swinging are called prehensile [pree-HEN-suhl] tails. Many monkeys, some snakes, and opossums are among the animals with prehensile tails.

Which animal sweeps or fans with its tail? Female salmon arch their tails, fanning the gravel in a streambed to make their nests, which are called redds. Here, they lay eggs, then cover the eggs with a swish of their built-in "broom."

Weapons and Warnings

Other animals use their tails for different types of survival activities. Tails used as weapons can be dangerous! Kangaroos lean back on their thick, padded tails and kick out when threatened. With a lash of their tails, thresher sharks kill other fish. Komodo dragons (the world's biggest lizards) knock down prey with their long, thick tails. Scorpion and stingray tails have venomous stingers on the end. Not only is getting stung painful; it can also be poisonous! And don't forget pony tails! Ponies and horses use their tails as handy flyswatters.

Certain creatures use their tails not as weapons, but as tools to scare or fool intruders. Rattlesnakes rattle their tails to say, "Get out of here!" Ring-necked snakes show the bright orange-yellow underside of their tails to distract an enemy's attention with false warning colors.

Some lizards actually leave their tails behind to fool an attacker. The broken-off tail continues to lash about, catching the enemy's attention while the lizard races away. This type of tail breaks off at a special breaking place, and usually a new tail grows to replace the lost one. However, the new tail may be different than the old one. Its scales might be uneven and it might have two or three branches.

Fat and Skinny

The final tail usage is as a pantry. Gila monsters and beaded lizards, which live in hot, dry, deserts, store fat in their long, heavy tails. When hunting is poor and the lizards go hungry, their bodies use the stored fat for survival. Some geckos (another type of lizard) also store fat in their tails. Scientists have noted that gecko and beaded lizard tails swell after the animals eat. The tails shrink gradually as the fat gets used up.

"Tails" of Survival

Fat storage, communication, defense, fighting, moving about, grasping, balancing... Animal tails may be at the "tail end" of the body, but they give animals a "head start" when it comes to survival.

6.4.4 Teens

Middle-school-aged kids (ages 12-14) and high-school-aged teens (ages 15-18) are capable of reading and understanding longer, more involved sentences and more complex words than younger children are, but kids of this age are usually not ready to read adult-level material. By the way, middle-school (or junior-high-school) -aged children are those who are in grades 7-8 or 6-8 in some areas. Don't confuse them with middle grade kids (grades 4-6).

The sentence "The me-first attitude of hippies, along with rampant illegal drug use, sexual promiscuity, and protest for the sake of protest that began in the 1960's with radicals in California, particularly in San Francisco, led the way into the abyss of the self-centered, blame- others mentality that continues to afflict baby boomers and subsequent generations that refuse to take responsibility for their actions and for their own upkeep" is not a run-on, but is definitely too long and convoluted for teens of any age. Sentences in teen articles can have more words and clauses than those for younger kids do, but young people in this age group will stop reading if things get too complex. It's best to use several shorter sentences rather than one super-long one.

Subject matter and concepts for teens can also be more complex and in-depth, but, again, keep in mind that teens are not adults. Articles about science, technology, culture, history, health, social issues, and relationships can tackle controversial and abstract territory, but most teens are not interested in many things that adults would want to read about. Articles about government budget woes, pension plans, or the latest household appliances would not be well-received by most teen magazines.

Teens do like reading how-to's and quizzes that help them deal with everyday problems they encounter at home and school. For instance, articles on "Six Ways to Avoid STD's" or "Eight Ways to Help a Friend With a Drug Problem" would be welcomed by many teens and teen magazine editors. The important thing to remember is that the advice must be well-researched and presented without lecturing or judging.

Teens also enjoy reading about other teens who have overcome obstacles or who have made a difference in the world. Often, such articles will motivate a teen to become involved in social causes or to think twice about doing self-destructive things. Teens also love articles about popular athletes, musicians, and young actors. Many teens spend time talking with friends about celebrities, and whenever possible, they attend concerts, sports events, and movies featuring their favorite stars.

Here is the beginning of a health article I did for teens. Notice age-appropriate language, sentence structure, the level of detail, and the use of expert quotes:

NEW WAYS TO TREAT SKIN INJURIES

Jared was slicing a bagel with a sharp knife. As the knife slid through the bottom of the bagel, it cut open his hand. Blood began gushing from the deep cut. Jared grabbed a towel and applied pressure, trying to squeeze the edges of the cut together. But 15 minutes later the wound was still bleeding. Jared's mom took him to the emergency room for stitches.

Jared dreaded the stitches. But, fortunately, the ER doctor had a better idea. "We can use a skin adhesive to hold the cut shut," the doctor told Jared. "It works as well as stitches do."

The skin adhesive used on Jared's cut is just one of many new treatments available for skin injuries. All are designed to help these injuries stop bleeding and heal faster, better, and with less pain than such wounds used to cause.

The Skinny on Skin

The skin is the largest organ in the body, and it is very important to properly treat any injuries to it. Otherwise, skin cannot perform its vital functions, which include serving as a protective shield against the environment. "The skin is your first line of defense against the outside world," says Debra Dannick, M.D., a professor of clinical dermatology at The University of Pennsylvania.

The skin guards against heat, cold, light, and infection. It also regulates body temperature; stores water, fat, and vitamin D; and senses painful or unpleasant stimuli. "It also is an aesthetic organ—it helps you present yourself to the outside world, and it gives important clues about the health of the rest of the body," says Dr. Dannick.

Each layer of skin performs a different function...

6.5 Magazines for Mixed Age Groups

Most children's and teen magazines cater to a fairly narrow age range—9-12 or 5-7 or 13-17 or 2-5 or whatever. But some list a broad age range. *Highlights*, for example, specifies ages 6-12. This does not mean that every article in *Highlights* is meant for all kids ages 6-12. That would be impossible, since the interests and reading capabilities vary so widely. Some of the stories and articles are geared toward emerging readers (ages 6-8), and still others are for fluent readers (ages 9-12). That doesn't mean younger or older kids won't read and like articles meant for children outside their age group; there is much overlap and variation in interests and reading ability among individuals, and these age groups are not all that clearly defined. But for the most part, if you're submitting an article to a magazine like *Highlights*, it needs to be targeted to one age group, and you should specify what the age group is in your query or cover letter.

Other magazines that list a broad age range do not usually target material to specific subgroups. *Boys' Life*, for instance, states that the magazine is for boys ages 6-18, but their writer's guidelines instruct authors to "write for a boy you know who is 12." Be sure to study writer's guidelines for any magazine on your "submit to" list so you'll know just how the publication approaches the "age-appropriate" question.

6.6 Checking Age-Appropriate Words and Sentence Structure

When you consider the age-appropriateness of words and sentence structure for any age group, there are a number of tools that can assist you. One good reference book is *Children's Writers Word Book,* 2nd Edition, by Alijandra Mogilner and Tayopa Mogilner. This book lists words according to when they are introduced in most schools. It also contains a grade level appropriate thesaurus that is helpful for finding words that mean the same thing.

There are also a number of computer-based methods of checking reading or grade levels of words and sentences. One is the Flesch-Kincaid Grade Level Score, which calculates a grade level score for a word, sentence, or passage based on the average number of syllables per word and the average number of words per sentence. Flesch-Kincaid is programmed into some word processing programs, such as Microsoft Word.

However, in my experience, the word lists provided in *Children's Writers Word Book* and the grade level calculations on computer-based readability scores have limited value. Some editors insist that writers use them, but many editors also realize that sometimes these tools defy common sense. For example, the *Children's Writers Word Book* lists "hungry" as a second grade word, but I know from experience that much younger kids can read and understand this word. The book lists "sparkle" as a fifth grade word, but my three-year-old granddaughter specifically asked me to buy her a shirt with sparkles on it and told me that her new earrings sparkle. She obviously understands and uses the word properly.

Of course, each child's vocabulary varies, depending on intelligence; place of residence; whether or not she has older siblings; and the occupations, hobbies, and interests of family members. Thus, leveled or standardized vocabulary lists do not apply to every child. Their primary value is that they present the grade level at which a particular word is usually first introduced in classrooms.

When using leveled word lists as guidelines, be aware that certain derivatives of a word may be appropriate for one grade level, while other forms of the word may be more advanced. For instance, the word "body" is considered to be a first-grade word, but "bodyguard" is a fourth-grade word, and "bodily" is a fifth-grade word. "Care" is a kindergarten word, "careful" is a first-grade word, "carefree" is third grade, and "careless" is fifth grade. "Music" is a kindergarten word, "musician" is fourth grade, and "musical" is fifth grade.

The length of a word does not necessarily influence its vocabulary level either. "Important," for example, is a first-grade word, but "impose" is a fourth-grade word. "Knowledge" is a second-grade word, while "lapse" is a sixth-grade word. "Monument" is a second-grade word, while "myth" is a fourth-grade word.

The context in which a word is used, along with the word itself, also influences age-appropriateness, and leveled word lists do not address this fact. If you talk about organic vegetables with a preschooler whose family buys or grows organic products, he will understand the word perfectly. But if you refer to organic or inorganic chemistry, only older teens will know what you are talking about.

Computer-based readability scores, as well as leveled word lists, often seem arbitrary and inaccurate. For this reason, many editors do not require writers to strictly adhere to these scores. I was recently working on a nonfiction book for six-year-olds about military vehicles, and my computer Flesch-Kincaid score for many simple sentences kept coming back at 5th through 10th grade level. It leveled the sentence "Trucks take soldiers and supplies where the military needs them," as grade 5.2. I contacted my editor and asked if she thought the sentence seemed too complex, and she said it was fine and that I should keep it as is. She and I agreed that sometimes the grade level scores don't make much sense. So, as with vocabulary lists, use readability scores as a guide, but recognize that computer programs do not account for all the variables that make a sentence or word readable or understandable for a child of a certain age.

Writer Christine Venzon finds that studying the publication for which she is writing provides much more insight into age-appropriate language than word lists and computer-based readability scores do. "I go more by the word choices and tone of the magazine or magazines I'm trying to write for. Plus, each magazine uses its own standard because it's written for a certain audience. Kids who are reading *National Geographic Kids* might be more familiar with a science vocabulary than someone reading *American Girl*," she states.

Anne Renaud believes leveled word lists and readability scores can keep writers from challenging readers to expand their vocabulary, and says that instead of avoiding some complex words, she relies on her own ability to explain them: "I am aware of my audience, and write at their level of interest, but I do not dumb down words. I define them in an age-appropriate manner."

Advantages of Age-Appropriateness

Gearing your subject matter, word choices, and sentence structure toward certain age groups is essential for selling children's magazine articles. Obviously, you will not sell an article about how to resist peer pressure to take drugs to a magazine for preschoolers, nor will you sell a piece about how to tell time to one for teenagers.

Age-appropriate language and topics, however, are not the only factors that make articles salable. Other methods of bringing nonfiction to life and making it non-boring are equally important, as we'll discuss in the next chapter.

Chapter 7
Non-boring Nonfiction

In addition to paying attention to age-appropriateness in children's nonfiction, there are other methods of making your manuscript come to life and provide entertainment for young people. Salable nonfiction cannot be boring, and contrary to popular myth, nonfiction by nature is not boring. As *FACES* editor Elizabeth Carpentiere states, "I don't understand how some people can consider nonfiction 'boring.' It's only boring if it's written that way."

7.1 Creative Nonfiction

One method of keeping nonfiction from being boring is employing techniques usually associated with fiction, such as using dialogue, vivid language, or placing readers in the middle of the action. Some people refer to nonfiction that reads much like fiction as "creative nonfiction." However, *Highlights* editor Debra Hess points out that this term can be misleading and can even lead a writer to cross the line between truth and imagination. "I'm not a fan of the term 'creative nonfiction' as it pertains to material for children. All writing should be creative and engaging. But the term 'creative nonfiction' often refers to material that is boundary-breaking or that takes liberties with facts. Children are still learning how to read and digest nonfiction. So breaking boundaries is just confusing, and we never take liberties with facts. We often use other methods to engage readers, such as using graphs, maps, and sidebars to provide multiple entry points and to break up the text," Hess says.

Different publishers have varying preferences about using creative nonfiction that structures the article like a fiction story, but all are adamant that any such stories remain strictly factual. Any dialogue must have really taken place and may not be made up. For historical or biographical pieces, dialogue can often be found in library archives of letters, diaries, and writings from the period, as well as in books on the subject. Dialogue for contemporary articles can come from interviews with the subject or from other primary or secondary sources.

Elizabeth Carpentiere at *FACES*, which primarily publishes articles about world cultures, likes seeing a creative nonfiction approach to topics as long as everything is factual. "Kids want to be told a story, so tell them a story—just make sure you have the facts correct. We often have articles about food or holidays in our issues. The articles are much more engaging if they are told as a story—a family sitting down to a meal or celebrating a holiday," she says.

Rosanne Tolin, editor of the online magazine *Imagination Café*, likes to see nonfiction that is fun and engages the reader in a variety of ways, and this can sometimes include creative nonfiction techniques. But Tolin emphasizes that crossing the line into the realm of fiction just to make an article fun or accessible is not acceptable. "I really don't prefer creative nonfiction," she says. "I like to see exciting—even funny, or punny—writing, but I readily reject nonfiction that has any editorial voice or gives animal human qualities, like the ability to converse."

In addition to using dialogue, creating vivid, factual scenes can help bring nonfiction to life and help it read more like a story. If you are writing about how certain zoos and animal preservation groups are protecting endangered tigers, for example, it would be a mistake to present a boring, encyclopedic list of facts about the animals and the conservation efforts, as in "Tigers are graceful animals. But tigers are endangered. Some people are doing things to help tigers survive." Instead, create a vivid image of a scene that depicts what tigers are like and lead into the issue of efforts to save them: "The female tiger's black and orange stripes rippled gracefully across her body as she sauntered across the fenced field with her two frolicking cubs. A zookeeper's truck appeared at the entrance to the vast enclosure. The tiger licked her lips in anticipation of the meal she would soon receive from the people who brought her fresh meat on their daily rounds. These tigers live at the San Diego Wild Animal Park, and they are part of a captive breeding program that seeks to increase the numbers of these endangered creatures."

7.2 Show, Don't Tell

Creating a scene like this one and weaving details into the article, rather than making a boring list, is one of the most challenging aspects of bringing nonfiction to life. Sometimes it's necessary to summarize a few items in list form to stay within allotted word counts, but whenever possible, it's preferable to reveal facts and details through action. Weaving details into action is an example of the oft-emphasized writer's adage of "show, don't tell." Telling merely summarizes or draws conclusions for the reader, while showing gives details that allow the reader to experience the scene and to draw his or her own conclusions.

For example, the sentence "Angie was tired from being sick" tells the reader that the writer drew the conclusion that Angie was tired. But "Angie slumped in her chair with her head hanging over her shoulder" shows the reader how Angie was behaving, and allows the reader to draw the conclusion that Angie was tired and sick.

Another example of telling is "Jim sat in the hard, uncomfortable chair for two hours." This is dull, lifeless, and tells the reader that the chair is uncomfortable. Contrast this with showing Jim talking about his experience, as in "My butt felt like it had been whipped with a frying pan after I sat in that chair for two hours," Jim said.

Sometimes, though, writers get carried away with showing rather than telling. Every transition or statement cannot show; that would involve way too much detail and minutiae. So use common sense. In the above example about Angie, it would be perfectly fine to start off by showing Angie slumped in her chair, and then to summarize what happened next without the minute details once the scene has been set. "Angie slumped in her chair with her head hanging over her shoulder. Her mom felt Angie's forehead and immediately said, 'We're going to the hospital.' They arrived ten minutes later, but despite Angie's condition, waited in the ER for over two hours."

Deciding when to show and when to tell can be tricky. I find it helpful to consider whether summarizing, or telling, makes a transition to the next scene or idea feasible. In that case, it is acceptable.

Back to the original point of this section—how to use showing rather than telling to weave details and facts into the action of the story rather than simply listing them—here is an example of how to do this. First, the list approach: "Bears are big, furry creatures that have sharp claws, a huge appetite, big teeth, and they can swim and climb trees." Now, here's a way of breaking up the list and weaving details into the action: "The mama bear's fur glistened with water droplets as she emerged from the lake where she had been fishing. Her sharp teeth held two quivering fish that she did not relinquish until she arrived back at the cave where she had hidden her two cubs. One fish apiece would not satisfy the cubs' huge appetites, she knew, and she lumbered back towards the lake to catch a few more. But then her ears twitched with the reverberating pop-pop of a gunshot, and she had to delay her fishing expedition. Her sharp claws helped her scamper up a tree to the safety of higher ground."

An important aspect of showing, rather than telling, is using specific, vivid words rather than vague, general words. Vague words such as good, bad, pretty, ugly, very, big, little, hard, soft, sad, happy, awful, came, went, go, stop and many others tell the reader about a conclusion the writer has drawn about something. If you write "The noise was awful," it doesn't let the reader know anything specific about the noise. Awful can mean different things to different people. But if you write "The screech of her fingernails across the chalkboard made him cringe," this shows exactly what the noise was like. However, it is sometimes acceptable to use a vague word if it is going to be explained. If you write, "Friday was a really bad day for Jenna. It started off with a call from her boyfriend," using "bad" is fine because of the context.

Another commonly used vague word is "went." The sentence "He went into the forest" is nonspecific (and boring). But "He rushed towards the forest" shows a specific action and conveys a sense of urgency. Would you be interested in reading more about why "He went into the forest?" Probably not. But "He rushed towards the forest" makes you want to find out why.

Another example of a vague, lifeless sentence is "The wind blew harder as the storm approached." It's possible to bring this to life and show a clear picture of the scene by changing it to "As the howling wind accelerated, trees bent helplessly eastward, while a gray army of corpulent clouds marched across the sky from the west." For younger kids, a livelier sentence might be "The howling wind whipped plump gray clouds across the sky."

The renowned writer E.L. Doctorow once wrote, "Good writing is supposed to evoke sensation in the reader. Not the fact that it is raining, but the feeling of being rained upon." So don't tell the reader that the wind was blowing. Show him how the wind felt or sounded or what it did to the trees or the clouds.

If you have difficulty thinking of specific, rather than vague words to use, consult a thesaurus. This is an invaluable writer's tool that will give a selection of synonyms that can be substituted for vague, boring words.

Try listing a specific word or phrase that better describes the following vague words:

Example: walk – saunter
Example: talk loudly – shout
go to
a building
pretty
quick
wide
a book

When incorporating vivid, specific words, be careful not to overuse adverbs and adjectives. Many writers make the mistake of using one or even a string of descriptive words in an attempt to enliven their manuscripts, but this does little more than add unnecessary clutter and length. If an adjective or adverb gives a clear picture of something, use it, but if it's just a vague label, such as beautiful, nice, cold, or heavy, leave it out. Also keep in mind that using vivid, specific verbs and nouns can do away with the need for extraneous adverbs and adjectives. For example, if you substitute the verb "burst" for "took off" and the nouns "flight" for "the air" and "crow" for "shiny black bird" in the following sentence, the need for adjectives and adverbs goes away. Instead of "The shiny black bird quickly took off into the air," write "The crow burst into flight." This is shorter and more vivid.

One of the most overused vague adverbs is "very." Sometimes it is effective for getting a point across, as in "Thank you very much," but more often than not, it is extraneous, as in "She missed him very much." This is better expressed as "She missed him terribly." Mark Twain aptly expressed the overuse of "very" when he said, "Substitute "damn" every time you're inclined to write "very"; your editor will delete it and the writing will be just as it should be." Twain also penned the oft-quoted statement, "As to the adjective, when in doubt, strike it out."

Good writing that employs vivid language shows the reader what the writer wants to convey as briefly and clearly as possible. I call this type of writing "bright, tight, and light." This means that it glows with clarity without being weighted down with extraneous words. Use one word instead of two when possible. Avoid redundant phrases. The sentence "He emphatically told Jean that she had the ability to be highly successful in any field that captured her interest" is full of redundancy. "He emphasized that Jean could succeed if she just tried" says the same thing in fewer words. But striking a happy medium between using descriptive words and writing in a sparse, bland manner is important. Some writers become so afraid of overusing adjectives and adverbs that they avoid them entirely, and this is not a good thing either. Use these words sparingly, but appropriately.

7.3 Active vs. Passive Voice

Another important aspect of bringing nonfiction to life is using active, rather than passive verbs in most cases. In passive voice, the subject of the sentence does not do anything; instead something is done to it. For example, the sentences "The car was hit by a drunk driver," "The use of illegal drugs is not looked upon kindly by law enforcement personnel," and "Kim's little sister was taken to the movies by her mom" are all written in passive voice.

In active voice, the sentences would read "A drunk driver hit the car," "Law enforcement personnel do not look kindly upon the use of illegal drugs," and "Kim's mom took Kim's little sister to the movies." The active voice is more direct and less awkward in these cases, and editors insist that writers use active verbs unless using them creates an awkward, less direct, or weaker sentence.

In "Many American cars are built in Detroit," the passive voice is perfectly acceptable because 1) whomever is building the cars is not even included in the sentence and 2) the sentence is specific and not awkward or wordy. Replacing this sentence with one that employs the active voice would not be necessary or advantageous. "Many American car manufacturers build their products in Detroit" is certainly acceptable, but not an improvement over the passive sentence.

But the passive sentence "The use of illegal drugs is not looked upon kindly by law enforcement personnel" contains a subject that can and should be performing an action, and the sentence is also awkward and indirect, so using the active voice in this case is important. Putting law enforcement personnel, who are the subject of the sentence, in the driver's seat with the active voice makes the sentence more powerful and direct.

7.4 Making Nonfiction Fun and Accessible

Techniques such as writing primarily in the active voice and showing rather than telling are just a couple of the methods successful writers use to make children's nonfiction fun, accessible, and interesting. Another commonly used technique is involving the reader in the article, either by taking him on a journey or by addressing him directly. Kids of all ages find it intriguing to be part of what's going on, and they respond by joining in the fun.

I have read several articles written by respected authors who state that directly addressing the reader is a hallmark of an amateur wannabe writer. However, I and many other writers and editors disagree with this assessment. I have used direct questions and other methods of directly addressing and engaging the reader many, many times, and editors have never complained. I used the technique in the very first article I ever sold twenty-five years ago, and I continue to use it today.

Here's what a few editors have to say about the practice: Marilyn Edwards: "It depends on how the whole thing is written, but no, I don't agree that directly addressing the reader is a bad thing."

Elizabeth Carpentiere: "We use this approach. I think you need to engage kids directly sometimes to keep them on their toes! Bringing them into the story gives them ownership of it and creates a connection that you can't form with a list of facts."

Rosanne Tolin: "I like it! I think directly addressing the reader is fine, and can give them something relatable."

Here are a couple of examples of how I placed the reader in the middle of the action and involved them in articles right off the bat. I began "A Look at Animal Vision" like this: "Imagine that you are standing in a green, grassy meadow filled with yellow, purple, and orange wildflowers. A plump, grayish-brown rabbit scampers from one plant to another, stopping frequently to survey the area, scarcely disturbing the meadow's peaceful silence. Does the rabbit see what you see when it looks around the field? The answer is no."

In "Reel Science Fiction" I also involved the reader: "Welcome to Reel Science Fiction: The Final Frontier. This is a voyage of enterprising knowledge. Its mission: to boldly ask what no man has asked before—can science fiction movies ever come true?"

Using humor and wordplay, when appropriate, is another method of relating to kids and making children's articles fun. In "Exercise: What's It Good For?" I started off with an amusing anecdote and mini-quiz to both engage the reader and elicit a chuckle:

"Sydney is having a totally awful day. First, there was her least favorite cereal for breakfast. Then, on the way to school, she fell into a huge mud puddle, so the school secretary had to call Sydney's dad at work to come and bring her clean clothes and shoes. When Sydney finally got to class, there was a surprise math test. Uggh!

"When Sydney gets home from school she decides she has to do something to make this awful day better. Should she

A. Go back to bed and get up on the other side of the bed

B. Eat all sixteen of the Hostess Twinkies in the pantry

C. Play basketball with her brother

D. Watch cartoons on TV"

Kids also enjoy quirky or unusual trivia, so including this is another good way of making an article fun and interesting. I did an article about funny animal group names and included interesting trivia about the origins and meanings of some unusual group names like a lounge of lizards, a gulp of cormorants, an ostentation of peacocks, a gaggle of geese, a rhumba of rattle-snakes, a murder of crows, an ambush of tigers, and others.

In an article about unusual trees, I included trivia about the world's tallest, widest, oldest, fastest growing, and deadliest trees. Trivia can be incorporated into the main text or included in a sidebar to capture readers' attention and interest.

Children are also fascinated by gross things, and including a few gross facts can add interest and even humor to an article. But writers need to use discretion about what is mentionable and unmentionable. Obviously, talking about the details of a sexual assault or giving an explicit exposé on an individual's toilet habits would never be appropriate. But in some instances, describing something like the gory and disfiguring injuries a person sustained in a drunk driving accident might be an appropriate way to make an impact on teens in an article on the dangers of drunk driving.

For younger kids, an occasional reference to toilet topics, farts, snot, or creepy crawly things can inspire a robust "eeew!" that will make the article more interesting. Kids are intrigued by these topics, and reading about them in a non-threatening manner can be fun for them. But refrain from mentioning these things just to add a gross angle to an article; whatever you include must have direct relevance to the topic about which you are writing. In an article I wrote titled "They're Baaack!" about the recent re-emergence of bedbugs in the United States, for example, it was natural to include a bit of an "eeew" factor. I started the article with "Sleep tight, don't let the bedbugs bite. For years, this was just a catchy saying in this country, since there were virtually no bedbugs in the United States. Now the creepy-crawly bloodsuckers are back. If you wake up with itchy red spots and see tiny brownish spots (their droppings – eeew) on the sheets, chances are you've got 'em in your bed."

Keep the "direct relevance" requirement in mind for other intriguing tidbits you may want to include in your articles as well. Length restrictions mean that you can't cram every interesting bit of information you encountered in your research; besides, editors do not want articles that throw in anything and everything about a topic. Editors want tightly focused pieces about one aspect of the subject. So before including a cool fact or explanation, it's important to ask yourself whether it relates directly to your focus. If you're writing about how dogs can warn people about earthquakes, don't be tempted to throw in something about how dogs also save lives by doing search and rescue, interesting as this fact may be.

7.5 Using Quotes Effectively

The same principle applies to the inclusion of quotes, anecdotes, analogies, and examples. All of these instruments can add life, flavor, and credibility to an article, but they should not be used just for the sake of using them or just because they contain intriguing information. It may be tempting to include a quote from an expert, for example, to lend authority to a point or even to demonstrate that you interviewed the individual, but unless the quote is directly related to the point you are making and is age-appropriate, resist the temptation. Also keep in mind that quotes should be used sparingly and briefly when they are employed. If a person you interviewed has gone on for two whole paragraphs about a particular point, pick and choose a relevant part or parts, but avoid using the entire quote verbatim unless it is telling a compelling story about an incident in the person's own words. A child or teen would find it tedious to swim through most lengthy quotes, and it also would probably take up much more of the allotted word count than you can spare for one idea or expert.

When you quote an expert or an article subject you have interviewed, the individual grants you permission to use the quotes just by speaking with you, unless he or she explicitly asks you not to quote them in a particular instance. But for direct quotes you wish to use from books, magazines, or websites, you must obtain written permission from the author or publisher in most instances. See Chapter 13 for details on the legal aspects of copyright law and the use of quotes.

It is important to correctly attribute quotes from any source, whether or not the requirement to obtain permission applies. For instance, it is not necessary to obtain permission to quote from a United States government publication or Website, but it is still important to correctly attribute the quote. This can be handled like this: Admiral John Smith stated on the United States Navy Website that "Our Navy remains committed to gender equality."

Some writers lift a quote from a book, article, or Internet source and do not correctly attribute the source in an attempt to make it look like the quote came from someone the writer interviewed. This is unethical and can also be grounds for a copyright lawsuit. If you use a quote you found in another source, credit the source. For example, if you did not interview Brad Pitt, but use a quote he gave to *The New York Times*, attribute it like this: "I don't think Angelina and I need any more kids right now," Pitt stated in a 2010 *New York Times* interview.

Also be sure that any quotes you use from any source are accurate and are used in the correct context. If you're not sure, ask the person you have interviewed. She will be glad to confirm that you got the quote right rather than being misquoted. If you don't check, fact checkers at the magazine you're writing for will check everything, and your error will come out in the long run. By the way, fact checking by a publisher is not a slap in the face or a test of a writer's credibility. Most magazines fact check everything, including quotes, for their own reputation and legal liability—so expect it and welcome it.

When quoting a source, there are several methods of attributing the quote. In most instances, using the present tense of a verb, such as "Joe Smith says" or "Joe Smith states in his book *Animal Tracks*" is preferable to using the past tense, as in "said" or "stated." But this may depend on editorial policy and on the context in which the quote is used. For example, if you write "Joe Smith opened the door to a new theory of animal behavior when he stated 'Lions know how to track zebra footprints' in his book *Animal Tracks*," obviously the past tense (stated) is correct, in keeping with the past tense "opened."

Some writers try to use fancy, overly descriptive verbs of attribution in their articles, but usually it's best to stick with "says," "said," "states," "stated," "explains," or "explained." Sometimes the nature of the quote or the intent of the speaker requires a more descriptive term, but these should be used sparingly. For instance, it would be appropriate to use the word "exclaimed" in "I really get tired of the rabid paparazzi chasing me around town!" exclaimed Robbie Actor in an interview, or to use "gushes" in Sarah Singer speaks directly from the heart when she gushes, "I didn't know it was possible to love anyone as much as I love my new baby!" Other times, using descriptive adverbs to modify "say" or "states" or any of the other usual attribution verbs is acceptable, as in "I miss my best friend so much," Brandon says wistfully as he wipes a tear from his cheek. But avoid overusing adverbs with verbs of attribution, just like you would with other verbs. If you use a string of descriptive words or even a single adverb every time you quote a source, this can get tedious and is usually unnecessary.

When using quotes, lead into the quote by placing it in the context of the issue being presented. This can be achieved in several ways. You can write "Different experts project varying time frames for the development of new space vehicles. According to Dr. John Jones of the National Aeronautics and Space Administration, "We hope to replace the Space Shuttle with a new vehicle within five years." In this case, of course, writing "says" or "said" is not necessary. Or, you can precede the quote with a "states" attribution, as in "As Dr. John Jones of the National Aeronautics and Space Administration states in a 2010 journal article, 'The government is making a big mistake by slashing our budget.'" You can also precede the quote with a shorter attribution if you have already introduced the expert, as in 'Jones stated in a 2010 article that 'It's essential for NASA to maintain its research programs.'"

An attribution can follow the quote as well: "Animal tracks tell us a great deal about animal behavior," explains Dr. Joe Smith in his book *Animal Tracks*. An attribution can also be placed in the middle of two sections of a quote to break up the quote. "Animal tracks tell us a great deal about animal behavior," explains Dr. Joe Smith. "They also give us clues about family and pack structure."

7.6 Examples, Analogies, and Anecdotes

The use of examples, analogies, and anecdotes can add authority, interest, and clarity to an article just like quotes can, but the same caveats apply about making sure these tactics are directly relevant to the topic and focus. An interview subject may have told you a terrific anecdote about how he met his future wife while injecting laboratory rats with an experimental drug, but unless the anecdote has direct relevance to your angle, leave it out.

An anecdote is a short, true story that is usually more detailed than an example is. It can be paraphrased or quoted, but should not be used as a substitute for facts. Instead, an anecdote should enhance the facts. In an article about a doctor who received an award for his compassion and encouragement of his young patients, for example, an anecdote could be used like this:

Dr. Bill Regan fights for his patients and encourages them to keep fighting, and many are eternally grateful to him for not letting them give up. Fourteen year old Dawn Hollins, for instance, gives Regan credit for saving her life after she had already given up. Dawn shares the story of how it happened: "I gave up on my leukemia treatment because it was so painful. I told Dr. Regan that I was finished and was going home to die, but he begged me not to give up just yet. 'Let's try one more drug. It's new, and it saved a ten year old boy's life just last month. I have reason to hope it can help you too,' he said. I couldn't resist those tear-filled blue eyes of his, and I knew in my heart that he wanted what was best for me. So I said yes, and now I'm cured."

An example is sort of like a short anecdote, but it isn't really a story; it's just an illustration and clarification of a point or fact. Examples are important for conveying specific, rather than vague information. Instead of just writing "It's important to eat healthy foods," give examples to add clarity and backup to the statement. "It's important to eat healthy foods. Apples, brown rice, and lean turkey meat are examples of healthy foods. They provide necessary vitamins, minerals, and protein your body needs to grow and repair itself. These foods are also low in fat and sodium. Many people who eat too much fat and sodium develop heart disease."

An analogy compares one thing to another, and analogies are especially useful in helping kids understand and relate to concepts. I touched on using analogies and concrete examples in the chapter on age-appropriateness, but here is another example of an analogy: "Blood vessels are like streets. Streets allow cars, trucks, and buses to get places. Blood vessels allow blood to flow throughout the body."

One short note about anecdotes, analogies, and examples: keep your personal anecdotes or examples out of your articles unless you are an expert on the topic or are writing a personal experience or how-to article. Otherwise, editors do not want to hear about your experiences. As *Imagination Café* editor Rosanne Tolin states, "I don't like editorial voice. For instance, [if you write] 'When I was in Alaska, I had the chance to visit the home of the polar bears,' it will lead to a rejection."

While we're on the subject of editorial voice, it's also important for writers to keep their personal opinions out of their writing. Many writers are tempted to sneak in snippets that exemplify or glorify their beliefs. An overly obvious example of this would be writing "Sam lost his license for five years for driving drunk, just like selfish scum like him deserves." A less obvious method of slipping in an opinion would be something like "It is essential that we stop global warming before it destroys our planet." This sentence would be fine to use if it is an expert's opinion, but not if it is expressing your personal opinion unless you're a certified expert on the topic.

Non-boring Nonfiction

Using quotes, anecdotes, vivid language, storytelling techniques, and involving the reader are all effective methods of keeping nonfiction from being dry and boring. Once you master these techniques, your writing will spring to life and capture the interest of the readers and editors you are trying to reach.

Chapter 8
Terrific Titles & Beguiling Beginnings

While using creative and lively writing methods is important in an entire article, special considerations and techniques apply to article beginnings, middles, and endings. This chapter focuses on detailing the importance of and relevant techniques for article beginnings. Since article titles are also critical for sparking a reader's interest at the very start, I've included information on how to come up with intriguing titles as well.

8.1 The Importance of the Title

An article's title is the first thing a prospective reader or editor will notice, and it can serve to capture his or her interest or to elicit a yawn and perhaps a "no thanks." The title is the headline that announces the article's focus, and it can also promise adventure and fun that the reader will want to be part of. "The title and beginning can be the things that sell your article and make it appealing to readers," says *Hopscotch, Boy's Quest,* and *Fun for Kidz* editor Marilyn Edwards.

Editors sometimes change a title to make it stronger or more intriguing, but more often than not will keep the title you submit if it's well-thought-out and dynamic.

Not all topics lend themselves to particularly dramatic or clever titles at first glance. For example, "How to Track Animal Footprints" might seem to be an acceptable title for a how-to article. This title certainly tells the editor and the reader exactly what the article is about, and for some people, this may be enough to draw them into reading the piece. But if the writer puts a little more thought into the title and changes it to "How to Be a Footprint Detective," this is much more intriguing because instead of just serving as a label, it promises some adventure and excitement. This title is much more likely to hook a wider audience into diving in.

Sometimes writers think of a good title before writing or researching a topic, but more often the title grows out of the research and the finished product. It's perfectly acceptable to come up with a working title for use in a query letter, but always be on the lookout for ways to improve it as you learn more about your subject. Your research may lead to a little-known fact that pleads to be in the title—and that makes the title unique.

An important thing to remember is that titles, unlike manuscripts, cannot be copyrighted. You can use a snappy title you've seen elsewhere if it seems appropriate, though of course an original title is usually the best option because it's fresh and unique and totally yours. But I'll admit that I once used a "borrowed" title—"What's In a Name?"—because it seemed appropriate and intriguing.

When choosing a title, keep in mind that some publishers prefer short titles, while others are open to longer ones. Read the publication to get an idea of the kinds of titles they use. In general, shorter titles are better, but that depends on the subject matter and the publication. I usually use fairly short titles because they're easier for children to digest, but I couldn't resist using this long title in an article I did on sea slugs that turn the color of the foods they eat: "If I'm Looking Purple Today, It's My Dinner That Made Me That Way!"

8.2 Wordplay, Alliteration, Rhyme, and Other Terrific Titles

There are many types of intriguing titles, and different writers prefer different techniques for creating them. My personal preferences include rhyme, wordplay, and alliteration (repetition of sounds in the first letter of each word or within words). I have a lot of fun with these techniques. You may have noticed my fancy for alliteration in every chapter title in this book. If you didn't notice, take a look. I put a great deal of thought into these chapter titles and had fun creating them, and I am hoping that someone will notice!

Here are some alliterative titles I've used in articles for children and teens:

"Telltale Tails," which I used in an article about how different animals use their tails, uses wordplay as well as alliteration, so I'm especially fond if it.

"Feathered, Furry, and Finny," was the title of an article I wrote about being a responsible pet owner.

"Autism, Actually" incorporates alliteration and wordplay, with a reference to the movie "Love, Actually."

"Addressing Acne Agony" was an article about acne solutions for teens.

Titles I've created that incorporate rhyme include:

"Fighting the Plaque Attack" was about tooth care.

"Get a Good Start with a Healthy Heart" was about heart health.

"Super Care for Your Hair" was about hair care.

"The Biggest Summer Bummer" was about sunburn.

Titles that use wordplay are especially fun to create. Here are a few I've used:

I titled an article about hair health "The Mane Event."

"Cybercrime Doesn't Pay" was about how the FBI catches cyber-criminals.

"Fitness is Par for the Course" was about the fitness benefits of golf.

"Lost and Found" was about an animal that biologists thought was extinct, but was re-discovered.

I titled an article about methods of keeping bugs away during the summer "When You Want Insects to Bug Off."

"Reel Science Fiction" was about whether or not certain things in science fiction movies could happen in real life.

"Don't Let Your Computer Byte" was about computer safety.

"Putting Your Best Feet Forward" was about foot care.

One of my favorite wordplay titles was not for a children's article; it was for a travel article for adults about Zion National Park. But I really like it, so here it is: "Zion in Winter." The reference is, of course, to the movie "Lion in Winter."

Writer Anne Renaud enjoys using wordplay and alliteration as well. She titled an article about a Vienna vegetable orchestra (yes, it really exists!) "An Appetite for Music," one on gargoyles "Stony Faces," and one on cotton candy "Fuzzy Food."

Christine Venzon also enjoys using alliteration, rhyme, and humor in her titles, and makes some good points about humor and titles in general: "I like to use humor, rhyme, alliteration—the same stuff adults find appealing. My article for *Imagination Café* on the many uses of processed potatoes was called "This Spud's No Dud." But I learned from my textbook-writing days, the title should tell without any guesswork what the article is about, so I can't be too cutesy. You also have to remember that kids might not get the humor as an adult would. The title has to be written for them just like the article. An article I did for older students on the Glencoe Online Learning Center on sourdough bread was called "Starting Something Wild." "Wild" refers to the yeast, but the teens picked up on the double meaning."

When considering possible titles, remember that good titles don't have to contain wordplay, rhyme, alliteration, or any other fun gimmicks to be effective, as long as they're intriguing and inviting. A provocative statement or question work very well too. Editor Marilyn Edwards mentioned a question title she particularly liked because it made her want to read more: "Do Snakes Eat Scrambled Eggs?"

A few question titles I've used are "What's Your Body Image?" "Exercise: What's It Good For?" "What's Your Emotional IQ?" and "What Is a Medical Emergency?" All of these titles let the reader know what the article was about while (hopefully) making them want to read more to find out the answers to the question posed.

Here are some provocative statement titles I've used or seen in various magazines: "They're Baaack!" "It's a Dirty Job," "Introducing the Mowbots," "Putting Holes In Your Head,"

"Chocolate—Friend or Foe," "Humor Can Heal" "Meet the 'Itis' Family," "Banana Thieves," "High-Tech Ears," and "A Chewable Toothbrush." All make me want to read more!

To sharpen your "terrific title" skills, consider the following titles and try to improve upon them:

- "The Best Way to Get Motivated"
- "Why Belly Fat Is Bad"
- "The Amazing Lizard Tail"
- "Time Travel"
- "Internet Safety"

8.3 Deck the Halls

Some publications require a deck as well as a title. A deck is a phrase or sentence that appears right under the title. It generally gives the reader more of an idea of what the article is all about, and can also serve to motivate him to read more. Here are a couple of sample titles and decks:

Title: "Conquering Fears and Phobias"
Deck: There are ways to deal with things you're afraid of.

Title: "Fitness Is Par for the Course"
Deck: No matter how you slice it, getting hooked on golf can have great health benefits.

Title: "Not-So Wacky Wake-up Foods"
Deck: Breakfast doesn't have to be boring.

Title: "Window on the Universe"
Deck: Hubble space telescope brings the world into sharp focus.

The deck is also a critical part of an article's "calling card," so give it some thought, just like you would the title. Remember that if you don't draw the reader in right away, she will move on to something else.

8.4 What Beguiling Beginnings Are and Are Not

Like a good title and deck, a good article beginning has the power to hook an editor or reader. Conversely, a less-than-compelling lead may have the undesirable effect of motivating an editor's rejection or leading a reader to move on to the next article. "I know if I don't draw in the reader with the first two sentences, I've lost them," says Anne Renaud.

So what makes a beguiling beginning? First, here is what a beguiling beginning is NOT:
- It is not wordy or complex
- It is not a definition of an issue or subject
- It is not dull
- It is not a summary of the article
- It is not vaguely related to the article's theme
- It is not untrue or exaggerated
- It is not a question that will not be answered

A beguiling beginning IS:
- Direct and uncomplicated
- Shocking, surprising, or just plain interesting
- Directly related to the article's theme
- True

Here are some examples of how to turn a weak or unbeguiling beginning into a strong one:

- This lead is wordy and tells too much right off the bat: "People who smoke marijuana, like sixteen year old Robin Dean of Chicago, often end up 'graduating' to harder drugs like cocaine, heroin, and methamphetamine, and they invariably regret allowing themselves to fall into the trap imposed by a spiraling drug habit." Better to start with a brief, compelling scenario so the reader will have an incentive to read more: "Sixteen year old Robin Dean hated being trapped in an escalating spiral of self-destruction."

- This "definition" lead is dull and evokes a "who cares" response: "Webster's Dictionary defines an addict as 'A person with a habit so strong that he cannot easily give it up.'" A better lead that indirectly asks the reader to care and relate would be: "Robin Dean never thought he would become an addict."

- Presenting a startling fact in the lead is good, but not if it's worded in a dry manner and does not really say anything the reader doesn't already know, as in "There are millions of teenaged drug addicts throughout the world." Instead, present the startling fact in a way that the reader can relate to and care about: "Teen drug addiction destroyed approximately twenty million American families in 2009."

- A lead that is vaguely related to the article's theme can misrepresent what the article is about. If an article is mainly about how a teen coped with his drug problem, don't start off with a peripheral issue: "California state legislators passed a new drug possession law in 2010." Instead, focus on the person and bring in peripheral details later on.

- An untrue or exaggerated lead may be attention-getting, but it's unacceptable when writing nonfiction. An editor will doubt a writer's credibility if the writer leads off with something like "Doctors at Johns Hopkins University now guarantee their patients that they will cure incurable cancers." Instead, be realistic and don't exaggerate. It can still be intriguing: "Doctors at Johns Hopkins University recently achieved a huge breakthrough that will revolutionize the war on cancer."

- A rhetorical question that will not be answered is pointless and misleading, as in "How many times do drunk drivers who still have their driver's licenses have to re-offend and kill people before the government will change lenient laws?" While this lead may inspire interest in reading the article, the question can't be answered, so it shouldn't be used.

- An extremely trite question lead is also not a good idea. Many editors say that writers often use a trite question in an attempt to draw the reader in, but that it's better not to use a question at all than to resort to this tactic. Examples of trite questions are "Do you like candy?" and "How many thumbs do you have?" Such questions are so mundane that few children will be motivated to keep reading. If you're going to use a question lead, be sure it's somewhat unusual and thought-provoking.

8.5 Effective Beginnings—Questions, Provocative Statements, You-are-there Leads

A question lead that can be answered or that is unique can be an excellent method of drawing in readers. Here are some effective question leads that I and other writers have used:

- I started an article titled "Putting Your Best Feet Forward" with the thought-provoking and informative question "What has 26 bones, 33 joints, 107 ligaments, about 250,000 sweat glands, and 19 muscles?"

- In "The Unseen Clock" article about sleep I began with "Have you ever tried to watch someone sleep to find out what happens?"

- In a how-to article titled "Travel Back in Time: Simple, Inexpensive Bath Products to Make the Way Your Grandmother Did," Suzanne Lieurance drew readers in with the question "Ever wonder what your grandmother did to make her bath extra special before the days of whirlpool tubs and Jacuzzis?"

A question lead can be combined with another effective type of beginning—the provocative statement lead:

- In an article on teeth, Fiona Bayrock started off with "Bite, nibble, chomp, chomp, chew, chew, chew. That's the sound of a mouthful of tools at work. Tools? In your mouth? Sure! You use them every day to eat and talk, and you show them to others when you smile and say "Cheese!" Those tools are your teeth."

- In "Wake Up and Smell the Caffeine," I began with a provocative statement and question: "Latte, cola, expresso, Mountain Dew, tea, cocoa, chocolate, diet pills, and Excedrin. What do they have in common? Caffeine."

- In "How to Care for Your Skin and Hair" I used a question combined with some interesting trivia to draw the reader in:

"Did you know:
  ✓ Your skin is the largest organ in your body
  ✓ One square inch of skin has 100 oil glands and 15 feet of blood vessels
  ✓ Your skin contains two kinds of sweat glands: apocrine and eccrine
  ✓ Hair is dead protein
  ✓ Your head has about 100,000 hairs?"

- I started "The Web of Deceit" with a question and a provocative true story: "Ever hear of the three women who died after they were bitten by a deadly South American spider that hid in a Chicago restaurant's restroom? Thousands of people read this online story, which supposedly appeared in the *Journal of the United Medical Association*. Guess what? There is no *Journal of the United Medical Association*. There was no such South American spider either. But anyone can post anything they want to on the Internet, and many people believe what they see."

- Mark Haverstock began an article about teens and sleep with a true story and a question: "It's 5:35 a.m. and Katie's mom comes in to wake her for the third time. Who says, "You snooze, you lose?"

Provocative statement leads that intrigue or draw the reader into the story can also be effective without combining them with a question. Many writers strive to begin an article with the most interesting or unusual facts they discovered about a topic. This is not always necessary, but when feasible it works very well. The important thing is letting the reader know that they don't want to miss finding out more about a subject.

In an article about the only carnivorous caterpillar in North America, Jan Fields drew the reader in with a hint that details about the creature's unique habits would follow: "Caterpillars are little eating machines. They gobble their way across crisp, green leaves, filling up for their amazing changes ahead. There's one caterpillar in North America, however, that doesn't eat plants at all—it eats woolly aphids. And it has a pretty sneaky way of getting them too." Fields comments about why she created this beginning and the effect it had on readers: "I used that opening to contrast what every kid *thinks* he knows about caterpillars (and what I thought I knew too before I discovered this little guy) with the reality of a carnivorous caterpillar. And I hinted at something even more unexpected to come, which draws the reader on. Kids *love* this article. In the times I've talked at schools, they grab up these [magazine] issues and just want to read it right away."

In "What a Kick!"—an article about RoboCup soccer—Mark Haverstock led with an intriguing quote to hook the reader: "You know they're robots, but you still scream at them," says Professor Manuala Veloso, head of the Carnegie Mellon University Team.

I began an article on teen accidents by drawing readers into a true story: "Shortly after midnight on August 4, 1998, 17-year-old Tara Jones was transporting nine friends home from a concert in her family's SUV. Fatigued by jetlag after returning from a trip to Europe the previous afternoon, Tara fell asleep at the wheel."

In "Clearing Up Those Acne Myths," I began with a yuk-factor statement kids could relate to as a way of hooking teens into reading further: "Whatever you call them—zits, volcanoes, pimples, blemishes, or acne—the thought of those icky white, black, or red skin monsters makes teens everywhere moan 'why me?'"

In "Really Extreme Hoops," I drew readers into a historical article by playing on the popular interest in basketball: "Thousand of years before Michael Jordan aired his first Nikes, Mexican and Central American athletes played a game very similar to modern basketball. While the ancient game used solid rubber balls on stone ball courts, it differed from the National Basketball Association in another way. A rather critical one. If the game was being played as a substitute for war or with war captives, the losers were killed—their heads cut off or their hearts ripped out, a sacrifice to the gods. Talk about sudden death."

Directly inviting the reader to embark on an adventure or placing him in the middle of the action is another method of creating a beguiling beginning. I began an article on water safety with "Summer vacation has begun, and you're at the beach, ready to plunge into the surf." In an article on computer overuse injuries, I also put the reader into the action with "You're sitting in front of your computer, eyes burning, hands and wrists aching, and neck screaming for a rest. Sound familiar?"

Off to a Good Start

Capturing the reader's interest with a terrific title and a beguiling beginning is critical, but a writer's work is not over once this goal is achieved. If the article's middle does not sustain interest, the reader or editor will move on to something else no matter how good the beginning was. The next chapter will discuss how to keep the article flowing so readers will stay on board for the ride.

Chapter 9
Magnificent Middles

After a good beginning hooks the reader, the article's middle must sustain interest and continue with a coherent, easily-followed journey. The middle, no matter how long or short, must contain interesting facts and anecdotes, even though the most provocative aspect of the topic may have been used in the article's beginning. Not every fact that is presented must be awe-inspiring, but they must at least be interesting and relevant to the article's focus. When going through your research notes and wondering which facts or issues to include, ask yourself first of all whether a kid would find the item interesting and age-appropriate. Sometimes something that is interesting to an adult would not be interesting to a child, so it's important to look at this from a child's perspective. Secondly, if you have been assigned an article and the editor has specified which points must be included, devise a method of weaving in all the required elements while highlighting the most interesting facts.

9.1 Flowing Merrily Along Between Ideas and Subheads

As you weave the individual ideas and elements of the story into a coherent whole, the article must flow seamlessly from sentence to sentence and paragraph to paragraph to sustain the readers' interest and to achieve the all-important goal of being more than just a list of discrete facts. Each paragraph must relate to and transition from the preceding one, even though a new paragraph introduces a new idea. This is what makes a story rather than a list, and editors say that the list approach is a definite turn-off.

"If an article is just a list of facts slapped together, chances are I will not use that writer again," says Elizabeth Carpentiere.

In all but the shortest children's articles (one page or less), it's best to break up the text with subheads that separate different ideas every few paragraphs. "Writers often submit long, drawn-out documents that aren't broken up into digestible pieces that are not only more appropriate for a young reader, but for the online reader as well," states *Imagination Café* editor Rosanne Tolin. But in most cases, just because you insert a subhead, it does not mean that you can abruptly jump from one concept to another without a proper transition. There are exceptions; for instance in an article that covers different examples that relate to the central theme but not to each other, it is sometimes acceptable to leave out the transitions because they would sound contrived. But usually, subheads are not an excuse to avoid tying the article together into a coherent story.

There are a variety of methods of insuring that an article flows from point to point. Here is an example of two paragraphs that do not flow and transition, followed by a way of fixing the problem:

"Debby's sadness began when she was nine years old and never went away. She often felt like she was drowning in quicksand because everything seemed hopeless, and she lost interest in things she used to enjoy.

"Depression is a serious disease that affects peoples' mood, behavior, and overall health. Some depressed kids just want to stay in bed all the time. Some start doing poorly in school. Others have all kinds of aches and pains."

Notice how there is no clear link between the first and second paragraphs. But creating a viable transition is not difficult:

"Debby's sadness began when she was nine years old and never went away. She often felt like she was drowning in quicksand because everything seemed hopeless, and she lost interest in things she used to enjoy. Her parents took her to a doctor who diagnosed Debby with depression.

"Depression is a serious disease that affects peoples' mood, behavior, and overall health. Some depressed kids just want to stay in bed all the time. Some start doing poorly in school. Others have all kinds of aches and pains. All, like Debby, feel sad and overwhelmed by life."

Just a few linking words, a brief reference to the previous paragraph, or slightly rearranging the order of the ideas presented in a paragraph can help effect a smooth transition. The same principles apply to transitioning between subheads. For instance, inserting a subhead into the above example and creating a smooth transition could go like this:

What is Depression?

"Debby's sadness began when she was nine years old and never went away. She often felt like she was drowning in quicksand because everything seemed hopeless, and she lost interest in things she used to enjoy. Her parents took her to a doctor who diagnosed Debby with depression.

"Depression is a serious disease that affects peoples' mood, behavior, and overall health. Some depressed kids just want to stay in bed all the time. Some start doing poorly in school. Others have all kinds of aches and pains. All, like Debby, feel sad and overwhelmed by life.

What Causes Depression?

"Debby's doctor explained that her depression resulted from low levels of certain brain chemicals called neurotransmitters. Low levels of the neurotransmitters serotonin and norepinephrine seem to be most at fault for causing depression. The brain needs these chemicals to help it regulate thinking, emotion, and natural processes such as sleep. Debby was relieved to hear that there was a reason for her sadness. That gave her hope that the reason could be fixed."

Notice how using Debby to tie together the two subtopics separated by the subheads made the transition flow into a coherent story rather than a collection of facts. There are other methods of achieving this; the first sentence under the "What Causes Depression" subhead could have been "Debby's doctor explained that the sadness, hopelessness, and other symptoms of depression result from abnormally low levels of certain brain chemicals." Either way, the new subtopic does not just come out of the blue; instead it grows out of the previous subtopic.

9.2 Varying Words and Sentence Structure

In addition to keeping an article's middle alive with easily-flowing transitions, another important rule to remember is that varying sentence structure and word choices is essential for sustaining a reader's interest and enhancing the readability of the piece. For example, it is not a good idea to use three consecutive sentences that contain three or more clauses. If you write "Dinosaurs, which roamed the Earth during the Jurassic era, ranged in length from turtle-sized to being larger than three elephants in a row," it's best to follow this sentence with a shorter one, such as "Scientists believe the largest dinosaur was Apatosaurus." This principle applies to all age groups, though of course material for very young children will not contain any sentences with multiple clauses.

Even when writing for very young kids, though, it's important to vary sentence length within the age-appropriate boundaries. Including a whole string of four-word sentences can get pretty choppy, as in "The deer ran away. It raised its tail. Other deer ran too. They understood the signal." Instead, combine some of the sentences and vary their length for a better flow: "The deer ran away and raised its tail. Other deer saw the white tail and ran too. They understood the signal meant danger. Deer tails can talk!"

As well as varying sentence lengths, it's also important to vary the first word in a group of sentences. A string of sentences beginning with "the" gets tedious. An example is "The blizzard swept in. The animals headed for shelter. The deer scampered to the forest. The rabbit disappeared into its burrow. The black bear lumbered to its den." It's better to vary the first word and to combine some sentences to make the passage more appealing; "The animals headed for shelter as the blizzard swept in. Deer scampered to the forest to seek refuge among the trees. A rabbit disappeared into its burrow. A black bear lumbered to its den."

Also be careful not to overuse certain words to begin sentences throughout the article. Using "there are" or "it is" more than a few times is tiresome. Fortunately, there are many ways of starting a sentence, and it is not difficult to avoid over-using specific terms if you pay attention to your word choices.

The same applies to over-using the same word within sentences if alternative words that mean the same thing are available. In "The deer ran into the forest. Rabbits ran to their burrows. A family of black bears ran towards their den," the word "ran" is repeated too often. Vary this by either using "ran" once or by using more vivid verbs in each sentence: "The deer scampered into the forest. Rabbits raced to their burrows. A family of black bears lumbered towards their den."

9.3 Sample Articles

I am including several entire articles I wrote that illustrate how these principles of varying sentence lengths and word choices and of creating smooth transitions between paragraphs and subheads work. Pay attention to each of these factors as you read the articles. I wrote "Lost and Found" for kids about 12 years old. It is quite short because it was assigned as a department brief rather than as a full-length feature article.

9.3.1 Sample Article 1

Title: Lost and Found

Deck: Although one rhino species is rediscovered, all are endangered. You can help.

The 3,000 pound black rhinoceros stood quietly munching leaves in the African bush. Suddenly a bullet ripped through the endangered animal's side, and it collapsed in a thundering heap.

Poachers, or illegal hunters, lost no time in rushing forward and sawing off the rhino's two-foot-long horn. Such horns are prized in certain societies. The poachers left behind the rest of the rhino as waste.

Rhino Rediscovery

Five species of rhinos exist, and all are endangered because of this kind of poaching. While the white, black, Indian, and Sumatran rhinos have been endangered for many years, the fifth type, the Javan, was thought to have disappeared everywhere except Indonesia until it was rediscovered in a remote, legally protected forest in Vietnam.

Although they were rediscovered, Javan rhinos still face extinction in Vietnam. This is not only because of the poaching and habitat destruction that exist in that part of the world, but also because of land mines and poisonous chemicals used during the Vietnam War (1965 to 1973).

The protected area where biologists found the Javan rhinos also may not be large enough to meet their feeding and roaming needs. Javan rhinos grow to be four or five feet tall and weigh 2,000 to 3,000 pounds. Animals this big require vast areas to roam so they can find enough food to satisfy their voracious appetites.

Because of these challenges to the survival of Javan and other rhino species, the World Wildlife Fund and several other groups like the International Rhino Foundation are working hard to make sure these creatures do not lose their battle to exist.

Armed Guards on Duty

One way these groups are working to protect rhinos is by helping to enforce laws that make it illegal to kill rhinos. The World Wildlife Fund, for example, supports armed guards who protect the rhinos from poachers in the Garamba National Park in Congo, Africa. Other efforts by this organization are aimed at political lobbying to increase the size of rhinos' protected areas.

Captive breeding programs in zoos are also attempting to increase rhinoceros populations. "We try to provide ideal conditions so they can breed in captivity with the hope of increasing the population and then re-releasing the animals into the wild," explains zookeeper Elliot Handrus of the San Diego Wild Animal Park, which has been successful in its breeding efforts with southern white rhinos.

Two Homes

Re-released rhinos are brought to the two places in the world where these creatures remain in the wild: Africa and Asia. Two-horned white and black rhinos remain in Africa, and two-horned Sumatran and one-horned Indian and Javan rhinos remain in Asia. Biologists and animal preservation organizations hope that with continuing captive breeding and conservation efforts, many more endangered rhinos will be re-discovered and someday will no longer be endangered.

The World Wildlife Foundation and the International Rhino Foundation say that there are important things people throughout the world can do to help protect endangered rhinoceroses. For more information, contact the World Wildlife Fund at www.worldwildlife.org and the International Rhino Foundation at www.rhinos-info.org.

9.3.1 Sample Article 2

Here is another article that illustrates important "magnificent middle" concepts. This article is crafted for boys age 12 and up.

Title: Really Extreme Hoops

Thousands of years before Michael Jordan aired his first Nikes, Mexican and Central American athletes played a game very similar to modern basketball.

While the ancient game used solid rubber balls on stone ball courts, it differed from the National Basketball Association in another way. A rather critical one. If the game was being played as a substitute for war or with war captives, the losers were killed—their heads cut off or their hearts ripped out, a sacrifice to the gods. Talk about sudden death.

The First Foul Trouble

Evidence from archaeological sites shows that the game was widely played by various pre-Columbian peoples. (Pre-Columbian means before Columbus came to the New World in

1492). These included the Mokaya, Olmec, Aztec, Maya, Zapotec, Veracruz, Toltec, and Mixtec cultures.

Archaeologists state that the oldest known ball court is about 3,600 years old. The lethal game has long since gone by the wayside, but a nonlethal version of the sport, called pelota mixteca, has lasted into the present time and is still played in areas of Mexico.

Our game of modern basketball shares the same basic objectives as pelota mixteca and the ancient game (except, of course, the penalty phase)—moving the ball down the court and through a ring. Some scholars have suggested that basketball's inventor, Dr. James Naismith of Springfield, Massachusetts, got his idea from the ancient game. But most experts believe Naismith knew nothing of it when he dreamed up basketball in 1891.

Hard to Handle

The primary objective of the ancient and modern games may have been similar, but the logistics were worlds apart. The old stone ball courts were not at all like modern basketball courts, except that they were built with bleacher seats for the spectators. The bleachers were richly decorated with sculptures of various deities.

The courts themselves varied in dimensions, from 80 to 200 feet in length to 20 to 40 feet in width. The courts were divided in half and featured either vertical or sloping walls. Stone hoops were mounted in the center of the sides of some courts.

The number of players and their attire were also quite different than those of modern teams. Each team had two or three players, who wore gloves, padding, and leather helmets for protection from the hard, grapefruit-sized rubber ball. Players were allowed to use their elbows, chests, hips, and knees to advance the ball, but not their hands or feet. Wood and leather yokes fitted around their waists protected their hips from damage by the very heavy ball.

Obviously, making a basket was not easy—how would you slam dunk? Often the final score was 1 – 0. After struggling mightily to make that one basket, the winning team was rewarded with clothing and jewelry from the spectators, as well as escaping with their lives.

Deadly Serious

Dr. Michael Coe, a professor of anthropology at Yale University and an expert on the Mayan culture, says the ancients played the ballgame as a way to communicate with their gods—not at all like the modern goals of having fun, getting some exercise, and entertaining fans. Sacrificing the losers, for example, was believed to please the gods, who would grant good luck and plentiful crops in response.

The ballgame was also full of ritual symbolism. The rubber ball, for instance, represented the sun and moon. Passing it around the court, according to belief, would encourage the real sun and moon to make their own daily treks across the sky. The game as a whole was viewed as a ritual battle between the forces of darkness and light. Sacrificing the losers portrayed the victory of good over evil in nature.

Even die-hard NBA fans don't take the game quite as seriously as the ancients did, and the stakes today are nowhere close to being as earth-shattering. Next time you see a fight among basketball players or fans, remember that the game today is a whole lot more civilized than it used to be, though there's always room for improvement.

9.4 An Article That Sort of Breaks the Rules

While it is important for an article to transition and flow across subheads in most cases, sometimes this is not feasible or appropriate. In the following article, which contains diverse examples of different science fiction movies that relate to the theme "can they come true in real life?" I did not transition to each movie, and the editors thought the examples did fine as discrete sections. In a way, this is sort of like making a list of applicable movies, but in this case it went beyond being a slapped-together list because each section expanded on an example and stuck to the overall governing theme. Studio-furnished photos for each movie helped complete each section to make it stand alone. Here is the article:

Title: Reel Science Fiction

Welcome to Reel Science Fiction: The Final Frontier. This is a voyage of enterprising knowledge. Its mission: to boldly ask what no man has asked before: can science fiction movies ever come true?

It Must Matter—and Antimatter

Beam us up, Scotty? Not so fast. The transporter device in the "Star Trek" shows "works" by taking apart the molecules in a person's body and reassembling them somewhere else. It's a convenient way to get where no man has gone before, but physicists say it's impossible.

The laws of physics don't allow matter to be completely converted to energy unless a matter-antimatter explosion is involved, says Temple University physics professor Dr. Leroy Dubeck. Matter is what things (living or nonliving) are made of. Antimatter is the opposite of matter—kind of like an empty hole in space. When matter and antimatter meet—boom! Why does this happen? Never mind. This explosion would kill the person being transported, anyway.

Look Out for Asteroids!

In "Armageddon," the government sends Harry Stamper and his oil-drilling team into space to blow up a Texas-size asteroid heading for Earth.

Good news: "There aren't any asteroids that big out in space," says Dr. David Morrison, director of space at NASA's Ames Research Center.

The bad news is that even smaller asteroids do real damage, so the tough guys may really be needed after all. It's also very possible that one of these smaller asteroids will actually hit Earth.

"A 10-mile wide asteroid is what we believe wiped out the dinosaurs," Dr. Morrison says. Chances are about 1 in 10,000 that there will be another catastrophic impact in the next hundred years.

If an asteroid heads our way, scientists believe we'll have more than the few weeks' notice the people in the movie had. There would probably be enough time to take evasive measures.

Still, Harry Stamper and his tough-guy oil-drilling crew might want to stay on alert.

Dinos Alive

Scientists in "Jurassic Park" grew live dinosaurs from DNA—the genetic code of all living matter—preserved inside amber-entombed mosquitoes. In real life, we do have the technology for extracting DNA from fossils and for cloning animals. But the researchers who study ancient DNA in amber (fossilized tree sap) find only incomplete DNA pieces, which do not contain enough information to put together a dinosaur.

"Reconstructing a complete strand of DNA would be comparable to writing a book from a bowl of alphabet soup," says amber expert Roy Larimer.

In "Jurassic Park" the scientists filled in the missing dinosaur DNA gaps with frog DNA, but that would be sort of like writing a book with a combination of English and Chinese words, Larimer states.

While research on fossilized DNA is valuable for studying the history and evolution of insects and other animals, don't expect it to lead to a theme park with real dinosaurs.

Flubber Falls Flat

In the movie "Flubber," Professor Phillip Brainard invents a gooey green polymer called flubber. A polymer is a long chain of molecules made up of smaller molecules. Polymers are elastic (they can stretch) and viscous (they can flow). Well-known examples are Silly Putty and high-bouncing superballs.

Flubber is different from other polymers because it defies gravity and enables people and objects to fly. Thing is, it just can't happen.

"Flubber violates several laws of physics and chemistry, so it isn't possible in the real world," says Dr. Dane Jones, a professor of polymer chemistry at California Polytechnic State University. "First of all, to defy gravity you would need a polymer that weighed less than air. But it isn't possible to make a solid substance with a density lighter than air."

Don't tell Professor Brainard this while he misses his own wedding three times to invent flubber, but a substance heavier than air could defy gravity only with an engine or other source of energy (as an airplane or rocket does). Professor Brainard's flubber, however, provides its own energy.

It's doubtful that the playful green goo in the movie cares about science—which states that an object cannot produce its own energy. But here's something to think about: Flubber could manage the feat by converting matter to energy—in a nuclear power plant or a nuclear bomb.

We're Gonna Go Back In Time...

The DeLorean time machine in the "Back to the Future" movies whisks its inventor and his friends into the past and future. So how about doing the same thing with a Ford Warp Explorer or a Plymouth Time-Bending Voyager?

Astrophysicist Kip Thorne and his associates at California Institute of Technology had a theory that time travel could be possible through a "wormhole." A wormhole—which no human has ever created—is a passage through space that forms the shortest path between two points. Picture an oblong balloon. To get from one end to the other you can crawl along the surface or you can bend the balloon in half so the two ends are touching. If you burrow a short hole between the ends, you have created a wormhole.

Dr. Thorne says time travel could happen if a wormhole—which exists for only a brief moment—were made permanent using an anti-gravity cement he calls "exotic matter." Then someone could enter the wormhole at one end and exit at the other end. The person would leave the wormhole before entering it, thereby traveling back in time, he says.

One problem: Physics tells us that certain forces moving through the wormhole would destroy it right before it became a time machine. "Time machines are probably forbidden by the laws of physics," Thorne says.

Call the Dogcatcher!

Don't worry, New Yorkers. There's little chance that a 20-story tall mutant lizard like the one in "Godzilla" will ever trample your city.

"It won't happen," says Smithsonian Institution paleontologist Dr. Michael Brett-Surman. "An animal couldn't grow to Godzilla's size because the bones and joints would collapse long before it got that big."

In addition, a 20-story-tall lizard would weigh 8,000 times more than a one-story lizard would. Such a large creature's skin could not hold its insides, and its legs would collapse if it tried to walk.

"A creature that big would also have to eat the equivalent of a sperm whale every day, so it would run out of food pretty quickly," Dr. Brett-Surman says. That's about 1.5 million fast-food fish sandwiches per day.

Muddling Through the Middle

Reading an article from beginning to end should not be a chore, and the most frequent culprit in leading a reader to lose interest is a middle that sags and makes getting through it seem like slogging through mud in slow motion. Keeping the flow going with effective transitions, vivid language, and the other techniques described in this chapter and in Chapters 6 and 7 will insure that the middle is an enjoyable and enlightening part of the entire nonfiction   adventure.

Chapter 10
Effervescent Endings

Just as a beguiling beginning is essential for hooking a reader and a magnificent middle keeps the person reading, a good ending is critical for leaving a memorable, satisfying impression. A good ending can also motivate a reader to pursue further information about a topic or to remember the author in a positive way and to seek out more of the author's work.

It is acceptable to end some articles without a formal wrap-up when the article is just a few paragraphs long; this short length usually makes a summary or full-circle or other type of ending pointless. Other times, an editor may request that the article end with a reference for readers who wish to pursue more information on the topic. This is not the most exciting type of ending, but if an editor wants it, that's how it has to be. For instance, I was asked to end an article on drug interactions with such a reference, so my conclusion was "For further information on drug interactions check out the FDA website at www.cfsan.fda.gov." But in most cases, a well-thought-out ending that gives a sense of closure is preferable.

Well-thought-out nonfiction endings can take several forms. Title endings, full-circle endings, weird endings, summary endings, quotation endings, advice endings, and significance endings can all be effective methods of adding a memorable conclusion.

10.1 The Title Ending

A title ending refers to or repeats the article's title, and is an effective way of making the title memorable and drawing everything in the piece together. In a computer safety article titled "Don't Let Your Computer Byte," I ended with "Your computer can be fun and can help you learn too. Just remember to follow some simple rules so it doesn't byte!" Readers most likely remembered the "byte" pun after seeing it in both the title and ending.

I ended a similar article called "How to Be Safe in Cyberspace" with the title ending "If you do find an online friend you really want to meet, be sure to meet in a public place with parents present. If you gain a new friend—great! If not, at least you'll keep yourself safe in cyberspace." Hopefully, the catchy phrase "safe in cyberspace" stayed with the reader.

In "No Nonsense Sun Sense" I ended with "Doctors have proven the benefits of avoiding UV exposure. You can do your part by remembering to follow a few no nonsense sun sense rules." Again, seeing the phrase "no nonsense sun sense" in both the title and ending made it more memorable and reinforced the message of the entire article.

Creating a title ending is not difficult—after all, you chose the title itself to be intriguing and memorable, and it should have relevance to the article's theme. Thus, finding a way to plug it in to a closing statement about any aspect of the subject you are writing about should be a natural fit. The title then serves as both the hook that snares a reader and as the conclusion that wraps everything up.

10.2 The Significance Ending

Many types of endings, including title endings, may double as significance endings, which allude to why the article and its topic are important. But significance endings do not necessarily include a reference to a title, and they can also differ from the other kinds of endings, so they are really a separate ending category.

In a teen article about emotional intelligence, titled "What's Your Emotional IQ?", I used a significance ending to expand the concept of emotional intelligence beyond its relevance to individuals and to highlight its importance in global issues as well: "While emotional intelligence is certainly not a cure-all for the ills that exist in the world, it is an important factor in many global and personal issues. Road rage, child and spousal abuse, and school shootings are just a few of the serious problems that raising peoples' emotional intelligence can address. Becoming aware of your emotional intelligence can be beneficial not only to your own health and happiness, but it can also help make the world a more civilized and peaceful place."

I used a significance ending in "Cybercrime Doesn't Pay" to highlight the fact that although modern computer detectives have a variety of high-tech tools at their disposal, the work they do is still similar to that of old-fashioned detectives. The ending went like this: "New tricks, such as rigging computers to destroy evidence and hiding data in image files, boot up all the time. That keeps cyber-detectives on their toes. So what's the solution? Just like the old-fashioned Hardy Boys, computer sleuths must keep digging for evidence and looking for new clues. That part of detective work is no mystery."

In "Thinking Small," an article about a dust-mote-sized spying device called Smart Dust, I concluded with a significance ending that left readers with a sense of how the technology may be used in the future: "Besides military spying, Smart Dust could help watch the weather, check on crops for farmers, monitor the temperature in buildings, explore outer space, and help parents keep tabs on their kids. About time to dust your room, eh?!" Ending in this manner was also intended to allow the reader to personally relate to the importance of the new device, so it did not just seem to be something with esoteric uses.

Suzanne Lieurance ended her article on how to make scented bath products with a statement about the significance of some additional perks of the products. The ending also contained a reference to the article's title, "Travel Back in Time: Simple, Inexpensive Bath Products to Make the Way Your Grandmother Did." The ending went like this: "When you've finished experimenting with all these products, not only will you find you've created some lovely gifts, you'll also notice your whole house smells wonderful! And, if you're lucky enough to have a bathroom with an old clawfoot tub like Grandma used to have, you can even travel back in time with an old-fashioned soak yourself."

Some significance endings give the reader hope about an issue or problem, and this can be an effective way of making the article memorable, as well as leaving a positive taste in the reader's mouth. In "How to Keep Bugs From Biting," the hopeful significance ending I used put a positive spin on the problem of bugs that bite, and in addition overlapped with two other types of effective endings: summary and advice endings. "While bugs have been known to ruin outdoor summer fun, a bit of planning can prevent them from driving you batty. Make sure you watch out for their hangouts, use insect repellants safely, bring along some emergency supplies in case you get bitten—and you'll have a great summer."

In "Clearing Up Those Acne Myths," I concluded with the positive, hopeful significance ending "So don't despair. Sometimes zits may seem hopeless, but thanks to modern medicine, there are many ways of fighting acne. And remember that most teens are worried about their own pimples and probably don't notice yours as much as you might think." The last sentence also doubled as an advice ending.

10.3 Advice Endings

An advice ending can be thought-provoking and effective if it is not didactic and if it grows out of the main point of the article. As indicated in the significance ending section, an advice ending may double as a summary or significance conclusion.

In a teen article on the dangers and pitfalls of tattoos and body piercings, I ended with the advice, "Remember that these body adornments are intended to be permanent. If you're not sure you want them forever, maybe they're not right for you in the first place." Hopefully, this ending got readers thinking about what they were actually doing when they got a tattoo or body piercing, which was the main goal of the article.

My article titled "Feathered, Furry, and Finny" emphasized the importance of being a responsible pet owner, so an advice ending fit naturally into the theme: "So before you get a pet, a family conference is necessary. Besides discussing responsibilities, your family needs to decide which pet is right for everyone in the family. Then you will be prepared to help make the pet's life healthy and happy, just as it will add much joy to your lives."

I concluded "Fitness is Par for the Course" with an advice ending that doubled as a significance ending, designed to get the reader thinking about how taking up golf might be of personal benefit. The ending went like this: "If you're already hooked on golf, you've probably experienced the physical and mental benefits the game provides. If you're not a golfer but are looking for a fun way to get some exercise while relaxing at the same time, consider getting in the swing of things. Tee time just might be the painless solution you've been seeking to improve your fitness level."

In her article on carnivorous caterpillars, Jan Fields ended with "So if you're ever walking in the woods and startle a small, wild flier, be sure to look for nearby aphid clumps. Underneath, there might just be a unique caterpillar enjoying its delicious, nutritious feast." This advice ending sort of doubled as a summary ending by revisiting several main points made in the article, and the advice angle also engaged the reader by informing him where to look for the caterpillar. Chances are that young readers will remember the ending if they ever walk in the woods!

10.4 Summary Endings

A summary ending, whether or not it doubles as an advice or significance ending, briefly reiterates the main point or points of the article without being overly-repetitious or detailed. This type of ending can be effective for tying it all together and allowing the reader to take away a comprehensive view of what the article covered. Be careful, however, not to try to include a detailed summary of every point covered. That would be repetitious, and the reader would probably skip over the ending entirely.

I ended "Telltale Tails" with a brief summary that also emphasized the article's significance: "Fat storage, communication, defense, fighting, moving about, grasping, balancing—animal tails may be at the tail end of the body, but they give animals a head start when it comes to survival."

In an article about people living with Tourette's syndrome, I ended with a summary of the main points and reiterated the theme that many people who have the disorder live productive lives, contrary to common misconceptions. This summary ending doubled as a significance and advice ending: "Anyone can have Tourette's syndrome. There are doctors, lawyers, teachers, actors, nurses, athletes, and many others in all walks of life who cope with the disease every day. Most people with Tourette's lead normal, productive lives, and many are very successful in whatever they choose to do. So if you have Tourette's, don't let popular misconceptions discourage you from being all you can." This ending provided a memorable impression about what the article covered for readers to take away.

I also used a summary ending in an article on the fitness benefits of running and walking: "Running and walking can be great lifetime fitness activities for everyone. They don't require fancy equipment, other than a sturdy pair of shoes, and you don't have to go to a gym to participate. Just be sure to warm up and cool down your muscles, take the proper safety precautions, and you'll be on the right path for looking and feeling your best." In this case, the brief summary reinforced the main points made throughout the article so the reader could leave with a comprehensive final thought about how to get started on a new fitness program right away.

10.5 Quotation Endings

Like a summary ending, a quotation ending can reiterate the article's main points, or it can double as an advice ending, refer back to the title or beginning, or serve to emphasize the article's significance. The reason for using a relevant quote to achieve any of these goals is that a catchy or poignant quote from an expert or profile subject can be more powerful and memorable than a simple statement would be.

In a teen article called "Addiction—Drugs on the Brain," I ended with a memorable quote from a teenager who had been there, done that. This person's testimony was far more powerful and memorable than anything I as an author or even an adult expert such as a doctor could have said to make the same point. The ending went like this: "Kicking a nicotine or alcohol or cocaine habit is incredibly difficult, but people who have done it know they did the right thing. In Charlie's words, 'When I finally tried to get alcohol and crank out of my life, it was the hardest thing I've ever done. I was in therapy for six months. But I had to do it, since the drugs were killing me. I had to get my life back.'"

I ended a teen article about the benefits of self-defense training with a quote for the same reason—no one could say it better than a person who had lived through the experience. This quote ending also referred back to the article's beginning and highlighted the significance of the main theme. The article's beginning was, "Violence. Bully attacks. Rapes. Muggings. These heinous acts happen everywhere, every day, to all kinds of people. How do you defend yourself against these sorts of assaults? Experts say that just about anyone can learn to respond effectively with proper training. Learning an effective response incorporates both physical and mental preparedness techniques." The ending included a quote from a graduate of a self-defense program: "As one female graduate of a Model Mugging class reports, 'Since I took the Basics course four years ago, I have often wondered whether the training would really help me if I were attacked, and especially whether it would 'wear off' after time passed without practice. I recently had an unfortunate opportunity to find out. On a running trail at a park near my house, I was attacked by a rapist. If this had happened before my training, I would have been paralyzed by fear and helplessness. As it was, I felt no fear at all. Instead, I was filled with so much rage that I became the aggressor. I think the assailant was totally shocked by this response—it scared him off, and I was safe."

I ended a children's article I did many years ago about Olympic gymnast Dominique Dawes with a quote preceded by some new revelations about Dawes that summarized pretty much everything I wanted to say about this dynamic young woman. The quote also gave readers insight into the fact that there was much more to Dawes than everyone who saw her spectacular athletic performances was aware of. The quote was undoubtedly more powerful and memorable than a paraphrased statement or a simple summary ending would have been. The ending went like this: "Dominique Dawes' willingness to help others while keeping up a busy training schedule and personal life is part of what makes her a true champion. She regularly takes the time to speak out on health, fitness, and drug issues, and she often visits schools to talk about self-esteem and perseverance. Dawes offers the following advice to kids about overcoming the obstacles that confront everyone, no matter what they strive for: 'I've learned to keep trying, even when I have doubts about myself. Set goals like stepping stones, so they're small and within reach. And before you know it, you'll get there.'"

10.6 Just Plain Weird Endings

Sometimes a quotation ending can double as a weird fact ending, and this type of conclusion can be effective as a nonquote as well. Just as beginning an article with a provocative or weird fact can serve to draw a reader in, ending on a similar note can leave a lasting impression that the reader is not likely to forget. This type of ending conveys a "last, but not least" message that can serve to remind the reader what the entire article was about somewhere down the road when the weird fact is what still stands out in the person's mind.

Christine Venzon explains how she used this type of ending in one of her articles: "When I did a piece on bread baking in ancient Greece for *Odyssey*, I ended it by telling them that bakers kneaded dough with their feet. It was interesting, fun, and memorable. Also kind of gross, which kids like. It left a good taste in the kids' mouth, if that makes sense." No doubt readers of Venzon's article carried a lasting mental picture of bakers in classic Greek attire with their feet in a tub of dough. And that's exactly what a writer wants an effective ending to accomplish.

In an article I did on methods of taking medication other than in pill form, I ended with a discussion of several innovative high-tech drug delivery methods being tested by scientists. Some of these methods were pretty bizarre, and concluding this way left a memorable impression about the direction in which medical science was proceeding: "Researchers are working on several new ways of getting drugs into the body, including a microchip that is either swallowed or implanted wherever needed. The microchip stores medicine in a tiny reservoir. It has a tiny battery and a microprocessor so it can be activated by remote control.

"Another new method uses electricity to force drugs directly into the skin. This process is called electroporation, and it can be used to treat skin cancers. Hopefully, it kills cancer cells without giving the patient the shock of a lifetime.

"In 10 to 20 years, expert predict, another new innovation will allow the clothes you wear to deliver medications such as antibiotics to be absorbed by the skin. Talk about a unique use of fashion, and a cool method of avoiding the bad taste in your mouth and the stomach ache that medicines you have to swallow often leave!"

In his article "What A Kick!" about RoboCup soccer, Mark Haverstock ended with some memorable weird facts about how researchers are looking into using remote-controlled robots in the future: "One project they're developing is a team of rescue robots—ones that would go in after natural disasters like hurricanes or earthquakes and search for survivors.

"Besides rescue robots, the researchers have another goal: By 2050 they'd like to field a team of robot soccer players and beat the human World Cup winning team!" This ending definitely left readers with something intriguing to think about!

10.7 Full Circle Endings

The last type of nonfiction ending is the full-circle ending, which refers back to the article's beginning to bring everything full circle. This is actually the most-used kind of ending. It is similar to a title ending, but instead of incorporating the title, it reiterates the article's lead. A full-circle ending gives a sense of completeness and closure.

In "Conquering Fears and Phobias," I began the article like this: "Darla jumped when the 'ghost' popped out of the bushes. 'I can't believe I'm scared,' she thought, heart pounding. 'It's Halloween! That's just someone dressed like a ghost!'" The ending was "'It's important to realize that phobias can be treated. Most people who seek treatment completely overcome their fears for life,' says the American Psychiatric Association. This is true even if your fears are worse than the usual Halloween jitters about ghosts jumping out of bushes."

I started "The Diet-Disease Connection" with "No one wants to get heart disease, diabetes, or cancer. Sometimes these dreaded ailments strike no matter what a person does. But did you know that it's possible to prevent some forms of these diseases in the future just by changing your diet now?" The ending referred directly back to the lead: "What you eat today can influence whether or not you get these types of heart disease, diabetes, or cancer tomorrow or even 50 years from now. The best time to change your diet to start preventing these disorders is right now."

Fiona Bayrock often uses full-circle endings because "I look at intros and conclusions like a set of bookends—they aren't exact copies of each other, but they match," she says. In her article titled "Another Alien Invasion," Bayrock began with "Green moist-skinned aliens with big, bulging, gold eyes are invading the west coast of North America. No, it's not some science fiction tale. It's a true story. The alien is a frog." The ending was "More study and close monitoring is required to better understand the relationship between the invasive bullfrog and native frogs. Meanwhile, the invasion continues." Not only does this kind of ending provide a sense of closure, but it also reinforces and creates a lasting impression of the main focus—the frog invasion.

In "Beagle 2 Mars," Bayrock also used a full-circle ending. The article began with "You can't beat a dog's ability to sniff out signs of life on Earth. Rescue squads have been using them for years. So, if you're trying to find life on another planet, why not send a dog to do the job? When the Mars Express mission takes off in May/June 2003, the time when Earth and Mars are nearing their closest to each other, the Beagle 2 will be onboard. When it arrives on Mars six months later, it will use its PAW to scratch and dig below the surface, looking for water and other signs of life on the Red Planet. Of course, the European Space Agency's Beagle 2, (just like NASA's FIDO), isn't really a dog at all. It's a sophisticated Mars lander, equipped with high-tech instruments and cameras at the end of a robotic arm, known as the Position Adjustable Workbench (PAW)." The article's ending referred back to the dog analogy, leaving the reader with an unforgettable mental picture of a space dog at work; "Beagle 2 seems ready for a big game of fetch. It'll be interesting to see what it comes back with."

Effervescent Endings

No matter which type of endings you use, the key to making them memorable is to think of them as an important final thought you would like the reader to carry away from the reading experience. Usually, just stopping abruptly without a more formal wrap-up will not achieve this goal, but putting some thought into a well-crafted conclusion will make it happen.

After you complete the ending, however, don't heave a big sigh of relief at being finished at last. There are still important tasks ahead that are essential for getting your manuscript ready to market to a publisher or to turn in as an assignment. Doesn't this job ever end? you may ask. Yes, it does, but not just yet.

Chapter 11
Formatting Finesse & Radical Revision

Before you send off your non-boring nonfiction article, complete with its terrific title, beguiling beginning, magnificent middle, and effervescent ending, it's important to attend to some critical details like formatting and revision. Such details can make the difference between a sale and a rejection, so they should not be overlooked in a frenzy of excitement about getting that manuscript sent off to an editor at last.

11.1 Acceptable Formats

Most publications do not specify a particular format, and in these cases it's fine to use standard formatting. This consists of double spacing everything except your contact information, which should be single spaced. Use one to one-and-a-half inch margins at the top, bottom, and sides and a standard five-space indentation for each paragraph. Include page numbers on all pages, and begin the first page with your name, address, telephone number, Email address, and an exact word count on five single-spaced lines in the upper left-hand corner. Then skip four lines before centering the title, and below the title type "By Your Name." Use a 12-point plain font like Times New Roman or Arial; never a fancy script.

Put your name on the top of each manuscript page, in case the pages become separated (pages should be paper-clipped, not stapled, together). It doesn't happen often, but if it does, having your name on each page can be a lifesaver. Editor Marilyn Edwards, for example, states that she has been unable to follow up on a couple of articles whose pages became separated because she couldn't figure out who wrote them.

Use only plain white paper—don't even consider using a gimmick like colored paper or 20-point letters to get attention. You want your excellent, error-free writing to draw the right kind of attention to your manuscript—not an unprofessional touch like chartreuse paper. "If your article is well-researched and well-written, you don't need to resort to gimmicks to get it noticed," Edwards says.

Some publishers specify a particular manuscript format that varies somewhat from standard formatting, and, if so, be sure to follow the directions listed in their writer's guidelines. For example, they may request that writers begin with name, address, phone number, and Email address in the upper right-hand corner of the first page, or that a reference to the rights being sold or the contracted date of publication appears with the contact information. Some publishers have varying standards for margins as well.

11.2 After the Text

Sidebars and the bibliography that contains your reference sources should appear on separate pages following the main text. Each sidebar should contain a title and word count.

Most publishers want sources documented using *The Chicago Manual of Style* format, but some may deviate slightly and use other formatting. Some may also ask for reference author's names to be listed first name followed by last name, contrary to the usual practice. For details on *The Chicago Manual of Style* formatting and on creating a bibliography, see Appendix B.

11.3 Letting the Manuscript Gel

Once your article is completed and correctly formatted, resist the urge to print it out and send it right off. Believe me, it isn't ready. It may seem perfect to you, but when you step back and return to it a few days later, you'll find all sorts of corrections and ways to make it better. I call this break period "Letting the manuscript gel." I cannot emphasize how important this is! You will catch typos, grammatical errors, poor word choices, unclear explanations, and forced transitions after you step back for a few days. You'll suddenly realize that you can cut out a paragraph without damaging the overall impact. This is especially important if you're over your assigned or allotted word count and you've been wondering whether you're going to be able to cut anything. At first glance, I sometimes say "No way can I cut anything and still cover what I need to cover," but after I step back for a few days, I see numerous places to cut and consolidate. When an editor specifies a word count, either in an assignment or in general writer's guidelines, she means it, and if a writer can't fulfill the requirements of the assignment, the editor will find someone who can. On a spec article, an editor won't even read a submission that is too long.

So, if you're writing on assignment, plan to complete the first or second draft at least a few days before your deadline so you can let it gel; then go back and revise and polish before you send it in.

Some writers have trouble acknowledging the fact that editing and polishing a manuscript is necessary, but successful writers know that nothing they put on paper or in electronic form is carved in stone until it's actually published. Even if a phrase or sentence or paragraph seems perfect in every way, it can, and sometimes should, be changed to make it even better. Isaac

Bashevis Singer was right when he said, "The wastebasket is a writer's best friend." Ditto for the "Open for Editing" icon on Microsoft Word.

Of course, this does not mean that you need to totally rewrite everything. When the famed Samuel Johnson wrote, "Read your own compositions, and when you meet a passage which you think is particularly fine, strike it out," I believe he was carrying the adage that editing is important a bit too far. But you get the idea—it is essential to examine what you have written critically, with a willingness to change or delete when warranted.

But some writers resist making changes, even after a gelling and revisiting period. Such writers tend to fall in love with their words, and they become incensed at the thought of changing anything. While love in interpersonal relationships can be a good thing when it comes to forgiveness or overlooking faults—it can help an individual forgive a spouse for snoring or forgetting an anniversary, let a parent shrug when a baby spits up on the couch or a teenager yells "I don't care what you think! I can make my own decisions," and keep a dog mom from taking her Labrador retriever puppy to an animal shelter after he chews up a whole wall of wallpaper and six kitchen chairs (yes, my puppy really did this)—it is not a good thing when it comes to being a writer.

That is not to say that you can't love writing or that you shouldn't take pride in what you've written. I love writing, and I take great pride in looking at an article I've written and revised and being able to say to myself, "I think I've expressed everything here as well as it can be expressed, and I see nothing more I can do to make it any better." But I also recognize the need to edit and revise, sometimes several times, before getting to this point.

I also keep in mind that even after I have determined that my manuscript is as good as I can make it, an editor may still see a need for changes. An editor has the right to make revisions on his own, or he can ask a writer to clarify certain points or tighten up a section or whatever. When an editor asks me to make revisions, I find it useful to view such a request as an opportunity for improvement, rather than as a blistering criticism of me or my writing style. Most of the time, these requests make sense, and I find that the changes I incorporate improve the article. Sometimes, though, I strongly believe that a certain phrase or sentence should not be changed, and if this happens, I politely explain the reason for my belief. The editor may reconsider, but if she still wants the changes, I go along with her wishes so as not to turn a minor difference of opinion into a major battle. After all, I am working for the editor, and we have the same goal—to publish the best possible article for the magazine. I also have another goal—to establish a good working relationship with editors so they will hire me again. Writers who are unwilling to work together with an editor on revisions will not receive repeat assignments. *Imagination Café* editor Rosanne Tolin sums up the consensus among editors that one of the fastest ways for a writer to get on an editor's "never work with this person again" list is to refuse to revise. "If a writer is not willing to rework a story (or seems offended by the suggestion), this will put them on my list," Tolin says.

Of course, if an editor tells me that he loves my manuscript as is and wouldn't change a single word, I am delighted, and definitely do not resent knowing that the job is done!

11.4 Revising After the Manuscript Gels

Going back to making revisions before sending a manuscript out, what should you be looking for after you have allowed the piece to gel? First of all, try reading the article aloud. This often uncovers grammatical errors and spots where an explanation or transition is unclear or awkward. Listen to the article as a whole, as well as to specific words and sentences. Does everything flow easily and naturally from sentence to sentence and paragraph to paragraph? Do the title and lead draw the reader in? Is your ending memorable and satisfying? Imagine your intended audience. Would a nine-year-old understand your examples and explanations? Is the focus well-defined? Did you provide enough details without rambling? Have you seamlessly woven facts with action and anecdotes? Have you supported general statements with examples and experts' opinions?

After reading the article aloud, do another visual inspection. Look for misspellings and punctuation and grammatical errors. Double check your notes to insure that any quotes you have used are accurate.

One thing I often find when I revisit a manuscript is that I have used more than one word to convey something that can be better expressed with one vivid word. I always keep in mind Thomas Jefferson's apt comment that "The most valuable of talents is never using two words when one will do." I think Jefferson was referring to verbal speech, but his observation applies equally well to manuscript revisions. When I carefully reexamine an acceptable sentence such as "He sorted through the debris in a painstaking manner," I realize it can be rewritten with fewer words that make it less cumbersome: "He painstakingly sorted through the debris." Or I'll realize that "This illness can affect patients' lives by making them tired" can be shortened to "This illness makes people tired."

Revisiting a manuscript also often shows me that sometimes sentences can be combined to cut down on verbiage. Instead of "Jeeps have strong engines, wheels, and bodies. These features allow them to operate well on and off roads," combining the sentences into "Strong engines, wheels, and bodies allow Jeeps to operate well on and off roads" cuts several words. Even cutting a few words here and there can tighten up a piece and make it flow better. Less is more, especially when writing for children.

Hand-in-hand with consolidating and striking unnecessary words, remember to look out for redundancy in ideas when you edit. Many times writers repeat the same idea using different words. If you write "Kids with asthma face many challenges" in one sentence, don't write "Life can be difficult for kids with asthma" in the next paragraph. If you've already stated that "Blue whales are the largest creatures on Earth," don't later write "Blue whales are bigger than any other animal." This may seem obvious, but it's amazing how many times I've caught myself repeating the same idea using different words. Only by carefully editing the manuscript do these redundancies become apparent.

It's also important to look for redundancy within a sentence. The sentence "Dr. Smith works at a hospital in New York and sees patients at the place where he works" is not only awkward, but redundant. It should be shortened to "Dr. Smith sees patients at the hospital in New York where he works."

Many publications pay by the word, but inserting or keeping extra words to earn a few dollars will decrease the chances of the piece selling at all. Every word, phrase, sentence, and paragraph must be necessary. At the same time, be sure not to cut just for the sake of cutting, and watch out for places where you may have under-explained a concept just to keep things brief. There's a happy medium between being too brief and using extra words. If you have made statements that are not supported by a quote, anecdote, or statistic, consider adding something to make the statement more clear or believable.

Over-repeating certain words or phrases throughout the article is something else that careful editing will uncover. Do many of your sentences being with "There are" or "In addition to"? If so, change them.

11.5 Other Editing Considerations

Another important factor to look for when editing is whether any quotes you have included are age-appropriate, relevant, and truly enhance the article. *Boys' Life* editor Brad Riddell says that he often sees manuscripts where a writer has put in gratuitous quotes, and he cautions against "including quotes for the sake of having quotes; not because the quote has anything of substance to add."

If a quote is not age-appropriate or if it does not really make the point you are trying to make, either paraphrase it in age-appropriate language or leave it out. For example, if you are writing for eight year olds, the quote "I encourage all my patients to brush their teeth twice daily to reduce plaque accumulation and to minimize acid erosion and dental decay" is way too advanced. It would be best to paraphrase like this: "Dr. Dan Dentist says brushing teeth twice a day is important. It keeps plaque from building up and causing cavities."

An example of a gratuitous quote that adds nothing of substance or that just repeats something the writer has already said is:

Bears head for their dens to hibernate when the weather turns cold. "Winter leads bears to their hibernation sites," says biologist Andy Animalexpert.

Either delete the first sentence or the quote, or use a quote that adds something useful, as in:

Bears head for their dens to hibernate when the weather turns cold. "Their internal clock tells them that food will be scarce, so they know they have to get into a deep sleep to survive," explains biologist Andy Animalexpert.

Besides seeing many gratuitous quotes in manuscripts, editors say they also receive material with numerous typos and spelling and grammar errors that conscientious editing would have caught. "I'm always astonished when I see multiple typos in a brief story. That shows me that the writer didn't put a lot of thought and time into the piece, and it makes me reluctant to assign to them again. Publications want writers who take their work seriously," states Riddell.

Current Health Teens editor Erin King emphasizes that misspellings, as well as typos, also make a bad impression. "You'd be surprised how often writers neglect to use the spell-check feature properly. I like to follow what I call the 'ophthalmologist rule.' Don't just assume that a word is underlined because it's too sophisticated or too specific to appear in the [online] dictionary. Check it! 'Ophthalmologist' is in there. I'm the greatest speller in the world but I always use spell-check, both to catch simple typos and double-check more advanced words," King says.

King notes another important consideration when reviewing and editing a manuscript—making sure all the elements requested in an assigned article have been included. "Sometimes, but not often, a writer will not follow the instructions provided in the assignment letter or contract. I think it's important for editors to be clear what's needed to make the story a success, but also important for writers to be unafraid to ask questions along the way, especially if an assignment letter is vague or confusing. If you're not sure about something, or want to run an idea by the editor, ask!" she says. Asking such questions, and making sure the assignment has been fulfilled, should be done before turning the piece in, and the time to catch these issues is during the original writing or revision process.

After you have edited for completeness and other details, do it again just to be sure you haven't missed anything. I try to put the manuscript aside two or three times before turning it in, and if I can't find any errors or better ways of expressing something at that point, I consider it ready to submit. But that's me, and other writers have their own standards. Above all, ask yourself—is this something I am proud to submit?

11.6 Getting Editing Help

Some writers rely on in-person or online critique groups for help with editing and revision. Critique groups consist of published and/or unpublished writers who provide mutual feedback to group members. I personally have never participated in a critique group because I feel comfortable doing my own editing. I would also hesitate to join a critique group, particularly an online group, because I do not like the thought of posting my work online for evaluation. What do I know about the group members? Nothing. I don't know if they are really experienced writers or if they have never written a coherent sentence. As an FBI agent I interviewed for an article I did on internet dangers told me, the anonymity of cyberspace provides a great place for scammers and criminals to hide behind a veneer of respectability, and no one knows who they really are or what they're up to. I'm not saying that people who join online writer's critique groups are scammers or anything, but I still don't know who they are. So why would I find their feedback helpful or useful?

I do read quality writer's publications such as *The Children's Writer* and Children's Writer Enews and find valuable tips on technique, editing, marketing, and so on in these resources, so I am not working in a vacuum—I just don't participate in critique groups.

But that's my personal choice. Many writers find online and in-person critique groups helpful and reassuring. For one thing, having an impartial party look at a manuscript and point out boring or wordy or unclear spots can reveal problems a writer has overlooked. A new set of eyes can not only help you see what may need fixing, but group members can possibly offer tips on how to go about making repairs. If you join an online or in-person critique group, you will also gain the experience of evaluating other writers' manuscripts. This can help you develop a critical eye for what works and what doesn't.

There are many, many critique groups out there; just Google "writer's critique groups" and see what comes up. Some groups focus on specialties like children's nonfiction, while others are more general in scope. Some have requirements for submitting and evaluating a certain number of manuscripts per week or per month, so the time commitment may be substantial. If the idea of a critique groups sounds appealing, you can always try out a group and see how it works out.

Keep in mind that while a critique group can help you step back and see what in your manuscript needs work, you are ultimately responsible for deciding whether or not the criticism is warranted. Don't expect a critique group to correct your grammar or word choices or use of quotes. Group members can point you in the right direction, but it's up to you to take the time to learn about how to fix these things yourself.

Rather than doing self-editing or joining a critique group, some writers elect to hire a professional editing service to make revisions. Most people who do this do so for a book, but some use paid manuscript editors for magazine articles as well. This can be useful, but expensive, and you might spend more money on professional editing than you would earn from the sale of the article. In my opinion, it's also better for a writer to learn to self-edit his work because sooner or later, a magazine editor is going to ask for some revisions, and it would not be practical to send out the manuscript to a professional independent editor for every little thing.

If you do consider hiring an independent editor, also be aware that there are many, many unqualified or downright dishonest people out there who claim to be editors. Many advertise online or in publications such as *Writer's Digest*, and anyone can pay to post these ads, whether or not they know anything about editing. Many writers get burned by scam artists whose advice is useless or who disappear without doing anything after the writer has paid them. So how can you tell whether or not an editing service is legitimate? Sometimes you can't. But fortunately, you can learn from other writers' experiences. A website called Preditors and Editors features lots of good information on complaints against certain writers' services. Another site called Writer Beware also has a good section on independent editors and manuscript assessment services, though it is geared towards book writing.

If you are considering hiring a particular independent editor, ask for references and for specific information about the individual's qualifications and experience, and check out the references. Also find out exactly what services you will be paying for. If answers to your questions seem evasive or too good to be true, or if the person makes any guarantees that you will definitely make a sale after the consultation, look elsewhere.

Self-Editing

With the tools you are learning about in this book, there is really no reason why you should not be able to do a competent job of editing your own manuscripts. There are no guarantees that the piece will sell no matter who does the editing, but if you keep at it and apply the principles you are learning, the likelihood of success increases dramatically.

Once you are satisfied that your carefully-edited article is ready to send out, be sure to make a backup disk or save it on a flash drive in case of a computer hard drive mishap. Carbonite or other backup services also work well. It would be a pity to lose all those hours of work because of a computer disaster!

Now the writing phase is done, and all that remains is the marketing phase or the process of turning in that assignment!

Chapter 12
Marketing Magic

If you are writing on assignment, once you have revised and proofread your article, you know just where to send it. Ditto if you've written a spec article that fits with a particular publication's theme list. But if you've written a spec article and are not sure where to send it, you have some homework to do before making a submission.

12.1 Submitting an Assigned Article

If your article was assigned, be sure to turn it in on time. If the editor has requested submission by email, you can send it on the due date if necessary. But if an editor wants it sent by snail mail, mail it early enough to insure that it gets there on time.

Editors stress that adhering to deadlines is essential if you want to work with that publication again. But occasionally, a legitimate reason for being late arises. A serious illness, surgery, or a family medical emergency or death are all legitimate reasons to request a short extension. If you are scheduled to interview a source and the person cancels or postpones the interview, this may also be a legitimate reason to request an extension if you can't find someone else to interview right away. A computer meltdown or virus that destroys your hard drive might also comprise valid excuses to be late.

If such events occur, it is important to notify the editor immediately by email or phone. The editor will usually be understanding if you explain what has happened right away and don't wait until the deadline has passed to do so. When you call or email, be sure to specify how much of a delay you anticipate. If it's going to be more than a couple of days, the editor may have to reschedule the article for a later issue.

Even if you have a legitimate reason for being late, it is important not to make a habit of requesting extensions, or it will reflect poorly on your professionalism and ability to deliver what the editor needs. A writer who claims to be sick one time, has a computer malfunction another time, and claims that an unreliable email server failed to deliver a manuscript on time for another assignment is not someone an editor wants to work with. It's a writer's responsibility to work around these types of problems as much as possible if they are actually happening. And a writer who lies and makes up excuses to try to wiggle out of procrastinating on an assignment does not deserve another chance.

In all my years of writing I have only had to ask for two short extensions—once when I was sick in the hospital for a month, and once when a scheduled interviewee whom I had contacted three weeks earlier cancelled the interview three days before the article was due. In the latter case, I had to find another source and schedule another interview. I immediately emailed my editor, explained what had happened, and requested a two day extension. She said of course that was fine, and I tracked down a good source, interviewed him by phone the next day, and actually managed to turn in the article by the original deadline because I had already done all my other research and had written most of the article. All I had to do was incorporate material from the last-minute interview before sending in the manuscript. The editor appreciated my letting her know that I might need a couple of extra days, and was delighted when I was able to turn the piece in on time. The moral here is that it's important to stay on top of things and not leave everything for the last minute. In this instance, the interview cancellation was beyond my control, but I had everything else ready and was able to tie it all up quickly.

In the instance where I was in the hospital, the editor told me to take as much extra time as I needed, even an extra two or three weeks. But when I got home from the hospital, I got right to work, even though I could barely sit up, and managed to turn in the manuscript two days after the original deadline. This editor much appreciated my efforts, and did not hesitate to give me new assignments, since she knew I would do everything humanly possible to meet my deadlines, even in extraordinary circumstances.

12.2 Submitting On Spec—Know the Magazine

If you do not have an assignment and are submitting an article on spec, several considerations are important when selecting the best market. First of all, study the market guide and any submission guidelines on publisher's websites, as well as reading back issues of the magazines you are considering, to make sure your word count, subject matter, and age group are a good fit. Editors say they regularly receive inappropriate submissions, and they do not appreciate it when a writer has obviously not taken the time to study the market. "A lot of writers use the shotgun approach and just send an article to every children's magazine they can think of. They haven't bothered to look at the magazine and guidelines. That's frustrating and a waste of time for everyone," says Marilyn Edwards.

Rather than sending an inappropriate submission, *Highlights* editor Debra Hess states, "The best advice I can give any writer about any submission is: Do your homework before submitting, and if you have any questions, contact us. We are always happy to answer questions."

Other important considerations in selecting an appropriate market include assessing whether the editorial and business policies of a particular publication are acceptable to you. Some magazines only buy all rights, which means that you can never sell the article elsewhere. Many writers prefer to sell to a publication that purchases one-time or first rights so they can later re-sell the manuscript to a magazine that buys second or reprint rights. (More on rights in Chapter 13). But some magazines that buy all rights also pay well and are prestigious additions to a writer's list of publishing credits. Thus, you have to weigh the pros and cons of each factor according to your needs and goals. Note: even if you sell all rights to an article, this does not mean that you can't write another article on the same topic for another publication, as long as the focus and details are different. But don't be tempted to change a few words here and there, call it a new article, and try to re-sell it. You can be sued for copyright infringement, and you can be sure the editors involved will never work with you again.

Other factors to consider are whether the magazine pays on acceptance or on publication. Naturally, it's preferable to get a check after an editor accepts a manuscript rather than waiting months or even years until it is published. But if the magazine is a good fit for the article, and if the general policy is for them to publish material a few months after acceptance, waiting to be paid on publication might not be so bad.

Many unpublished writers also consider sending material to non-paying markets just to garner some publishing credits to cite in a query letter, and there is nothing wrong with this practice if it fits with an individual's goals. But keep in mind that even publications that provide no compensation may have high standards for the material they accept, so it may not be as easy as you might think to be published in these markets. Always send in your best work, even if you're not being paid for it. An editor at a paying market might even see something you wrote for a non-paying market and ask you to write for the paying publication!

Besides considering paying versus nonpaying markets, another thing to think about is the amount of compensation the paying markets offer. It is natural to want to be published in the higher-paying publications, but the competition for these markets is also more intense, so it is often more realistic to start out submitting based on how well your manuscript fits into a publication rather than on how much the magazine pays. That said, it is possible for beginning writers to be published in higher-paying magazines if the article is outstanding, so don't discount these markets if they seem like a good fit for your material.

One mistake many writers make is tailoring the quality of their work to the amount of financial compensation expected. I have been published in magazines that pay anywhere from $30 to $1500 for an article, but no matter what the pay is, I always send in my best work. I would be horrified to have my name on something that was less than what I consider to be excellent quality. For me it's about being proud of what I do and maintaining a reputation for excellence, as well as being about earning money.

Besides financial considerations, another factor to think about in selecting a market is the average length of time a publisher takes to respond to submissions. Some editors try to respond within a couple of weeks, though this is unusual. Most often, receiving a response takes anywhere from one to six months. If you keep busy with new projects, waiting for an answer is not so difficult, but even so, it's always nicer to hear back sooner rather than later. If this is important to you, try to avoid sending your manuscripts to publishers that list long response times.

Market guides also detail the number of freelance submissions each publication publishes each year. This can further help you determine where to send your work. Obviously, a magazine that is mostly staff-written and publishes only two freelance articles a year is much less likely to purchase your manuscript than one that publishes a hundred freelance submissions is. You can also find out what percentage of the published articles is written by previously unpublished writers. While many magazines will publish an excellent manuscript whether or not the author is previously published, it does help to know which ones are likely to do so.

12.3 Submitting the Article

Once you decide where to submit your manuscript, pay attention to the magazine's submission policies. Some accept email submissions, while others require that the article be sent by snail mail. Email, of course, is easier and saves postage fees, and if this is an option, don't forget to include a brief, professional cover letter just like you would with a snail mail submission. Also be sure to follow publisher guidelines concerning email attachments. Some publications will not open attachments, so the manuscript must be pasted into the body of the email. Some will not accept certain types of attachments, such as docx documents.

For snail mail submissions, include a signed cover letter, paper clip the pages of the manuscript together, and include a self-addressed, stamped envelope (SASE) for the editor's response and for return of the article if it is rejected. It is acceptable to include a business-sized SASE with only enough first-class postage for a response notice if you do not need to have the manuscript returned (it's cheaper to print out another copy of the manuscript to send elsewhere than to pay for return postage). If you do this, be sure to mention it in your cover letter, and the editor will then discard the article if it is being rejected.

Enclose the cover letter, manuscript, and SASE unfolded in a 9x12 or 10x13 envelope. Be sure to weigh the package at the post office so the postage used will be correct. If the article is very short, it is usually acceptable to fold everything and send it in a business-sized 4 1/8 x 9 ½ inch envelope, as long as editorial policy does not prohibit this. One first-class stamp pays for up to five pages in an envelope of this size.

Send submissions by first class mail—some writers try to send material by certified or registered mail, but most publishers will not sign for or accept anything sent this way.

Some publishers will send back a self-addressed, stamped postcard to acknowledge receipt of a submission if you request it, so consider enclosing one if you want confirmation of receipt.

12.4 Photos

When sending a spec article, it's usually not a good idea to enclose photos, either in a snail mail or emailed submission, but it is important to mention the availability of photos in your cover letter so the editor can ask for them later on. Sometimes the availability of good photos will make the difference between an acceptance and a rejection.

Some publishers, however, do encourage writers to send photos when they submit the article. Marilyn Edwards of *Hopscotch, Boy's Quest,* and *Fun for Kidz* is one editor who loves getting high-quality photos with a submission. "One writer who's a fantastic photographer sends outstanding photos with her articles, plus she writes well and her articles fit our themes, so we always use what she sends. Good photos are an extra bonus, but don't send bad photos," Edwards says.

Good photos must be high-resolution (hint: cell phone camera photos are *not* acceptable) digital quality. Some publishers accept slides or high quality prints as well. If you have a decent camera and are a competent photographer, there's a good chance your photos will work. But in many cases, you have to rely on other sources for photos. If you're doing an article on tigers, for example, you probably won't be able to take photos unless you're traveling to Asia or Africa or visiting a wild animal park. If you're writing a history article, you'll also have to rely on photos from other sources. Finding such sources is not difficult. First of all, many people you interview can provide photos, so be sure to ask. I've gotten permission to use photos from zoos, museums, historical societies, celebrity publicists, movie studios, athletes, government agencies like NASA, and so on. Most of these sources simply require that the magazine credits the source when the photos are published. Some organizations charge for the use of photos, and some editors have a photo budget to pay for such photos. Most editors, however, do not do this, so it's best to try to track down free photos. Unless you have written permission, do not try to use photos taken by professional photographers or lifted from websites, other than U.S. government Websites, or you can be sued.

12.5 Cover Letters

The cover letter for a spec article should include not only a reference to photo availability, but also a brief statement about the fact that you are submitting the article for consideration, the intended audience, a comment that shows you have studied the magazine, and your qualifications and previous publications, if relevant. If you are turning in an assignment or sending a manuscript which an editor expressed an interest in seeing on spec, let the editor know about these circumstances.

It is best to address a cover letter and envelope to a particular editor, but some publications specify that all unsolicited submissions should be sent to a "Manuscript Coordinator" or to the "Submissions Editor." In such cases, it is acceptable to follow this request.

The cover letter should be single-spaced on plain white paper or letterhead stationery, and, as with a query letter, error-free and professional. No self-aggrandizement, such as "I'm sure you will agree that I'm a first-rate writer" or "I know you'll love my article." No threats like "You'll regret it if you don't buy my story." Writers actually do write things like this in their letters. What were they thinking? No revelations such as "This article has been rejected by fifteen other editors, but I'm sure you'll have the good sense to see its merits." Never mention previous rejections. Never mention that your kids or grandkids loved the article. *Be professional!*

Here is a sample cover letter for turning in an assignment:

Your address
Phone number
Email address

The Date

Jim Jaspar, Editor
Kid Stuff
1234 Main Street
Jacksonville, FL 54321

Dear Mr. Jaspar,

I am sending "The Last Chance" as per your assignment letter of March 4, 2010. The manuscript is attached as a Word document, and I have also attached two jpeg photo files showing Tim Smith and his teammates. The bibliography follows the main text.

Please let me know if you have any questions or comments.

Sincerely,
Annie Author

Here is a sample cover letter for an article which an editor has expressed an interest in seeing on spec:

Your address
Phone number
Email address

The Date

Jim Jaspar, Editor
Kid Stuff
1234 Main Street
Jacksonville, FL 54321

Dear Mr. Jaspar:

I am enclosing my article of 835 words titled "The Last Chance," about baseball legend Tim Smith. You expressed an interest in seeing this article in your letter of March 14, 2011. My bibliography of reference sources follows the main text, and I can furnish photographs from the Baseball Hall of Fame if you are interested.

Thank you for considering "The Last Chance" for publication. Please use the enclosed SASE to let me know whether or not the article meets your editorial needs.

Sincerely,

Annie Author

If you are sending an article on spec with no previous correspondence with the editor, the cover letter can look like this:

Your address
Phone number
Email address

The Date

Jim Jaspar, Editor
Kid Stuff
1234 Main Street
Jacksonville, FL 54321

Dear Mr. Jaspar:

I am sending my children's nonfiction article of 835 words titled "The Last Chance" for your consideration. The manuscript is geared towards your target audience of readers ages 7-10, and shares the inspiring story of baseball legend Tim Smith. My bibliography of reference sources and a brief sidebar on Smith's baseball stats follow the main text. I have obtained permission to use two photos from the Baseball Hall of Fame that I can send along if you are interested.

I have published numerous children's articles in magazines such as *Boy's Quest, Ladybug,* and *Highlights*.

Thank you for considering "The Last Chance" for publication in *Kid Stuff*. A SASE is enclosed for your response.

Sincerely,

Annie Author

12.6 Exclusive Submissions

Keep in mind that unless you state otherwise, editors will assume that you are submitting an article exclusively to their publication. In fact, most magazines require exclusive submissions. A few do allow simultaneous submissions to other publications, and if you do this, it is important to let the editor know in your cover letter.

Although most writer's guidelines expressly prohibit simultaneous submissions, some writers do this anyway without informing anyone. Writers who do this justify the practice by claiming that they want to maximize their chances of making a sale, and that waiting two or three or six months for an editor's response is too long to sit idly by and wait. I understand this reasoning—waiting for a response can seem like forever, and submitting simultaneously to more than one publisher ups the chances of the manuscript selling sooner rather than later. But I don't recommend doing this unless the publication states that they allow it. A writer who does this will not get caught if the manuscript is rejected by everyone, but what if two editors accept the story? The writer would have to inform one of the editors that the piece was already sold, and that editor would never work with that writer again. Publishers have reasons for no simultaneous submissions policies, and there may be adverse consequences for violating these policies.

In addition to only submitting to one publisher at a time, it's also important not to send more than one manuscript at a time to a given editor. Some writers include two, three, or more stories in a package in hopes that one will sell, but editors do not want to see multiple submissions. You can always send other manuscripts later on, whether you receive an acceptance or a rejection on one submission. If you receive an acceptance or a personalized rejection that encourages you to submit other material in the future, by all means make a note to send in something else if it fits the market, and remind the editor in your cover letter that she invited you to send in other material. But make sure other articles you submit are right for the publication—don't send a science article you have sitting around to a history magazine just because an editor encouraged you to submit in the future.

12.7 Keeping Records

It's important to keep careful track of any manuscript submissions, as well as queries, that you make, along with details about publishers' responses. Some writers prefer to create a computer file or spreadsheet for this purpose, while others use file cards or notebooks. I use several loose-leaf notebooks to track all of my submissions and published works, plus I keep a computer file listing all my published credits. In one loose-leaf notebook, the "active" notebook, I make a page for each query letter or manuscript and include the title, dates and places of submission, dates of any follow-up correspondence and editors' responses, and a notation about the nature of the response—acceptance, form rejection, or personalized rejection. When I receive an acceptance, I document the date when I sign a contract and list any deadlines or revision requests. I also list the date I send in an invoice if one is required, date and amount of payment received, and rights sold. When the article is published, I note the date of publication and also add the title and details about where it was published to a list of published works I keep in another notebook and on a computer file.

After a manuscript is published and payment received, I move the sheet of paper from the "active" notebook to another notebook I call the "finished" notebook. That way, I have a permanent record for each project for future reference and for financial record-keeping. This system works for me, and other systems work for other individuals. The important thing is to find a system that allows you to keep track of all submissions and publications.

12.8 After the Manuscript is Sent

After you've logged the submission and sent off the package, it will probably seem like forever as you wait for a response, but waiting patiently is part of being a writer. It helps to keep busy with new projects—that way you won't obsess about one manuscript. Many successful writers have five, ten, twenty, or even thirty manuscripts or query letters circulating at once or in various stages of planning, research, writing, and revision.

As you wait patiently for a response, it does help to understand why it usually takes awhile. Editor Marilyn Edwards explains what happens to submissions at *Hopscotch*, *Boy's Quest*, and *Fun for Kidz*: "When an article comes in, the first reader who looks at it knows pretty much whether or not it might work for us. If not, it's sent back [to the author] right away. But if the first reader thinks it has possibilities, it moves up the chain of editors. We check whether it duplicates anything we already have and decide if it's really something we can use. I make the final decision, and that can take awhile because I'm also busy with getting out upcoming issues and other things."

Different publications have different procedures, but most have large "slush piles" (stacks of unsolicited manuscripts) of hundreds of submissions, so it can take some time before a first reader even makes a preliminary assessment. Some magazines do not use first readers, and some send out unsolicited submissions to independent first readers. Some, such as *Highlights*, have different policies for fiction and nonfiction submissions. "Nonfiction submissions are routed directly to an editor, while fiction submissions go to a first reader," explains *Highlights* editor Debra Hess. So submitting nonfiction rather than fiction to *Highlights* not only means your chances of publication are greater, but it can also cut down on the response time!

However long a response takes, it is important not to pester editors about the status of your manuscript. Some writers call or email repeatedly to ask whether the submission was received or what is being done with it, and editors cannot respond to such demands for information. It is impossible to keep track of where hundreds of submissions are at a given moment.

That said, if the publication's stated response time has passed, give it a few extra weeks, and then it is perfectly acceptable to inquire about the manuscript's status by snail mail or even by email. Here is a sample follow-up inquiry letter:

Your address
Phone number
Email address

The Date

Jane Jones, Editor
Children's Health
1234 West Avenue
New York, NY 54321

Dear Ms. Jones:

On January 14, 2009 I submitted an article titled "Achoo" accompanied by a SASE. I have not yet received a response and am wondering whether you received the manuscript. If so, can you please check on the status for me? If not, please let me know so I can re-submit.

I would appreciate a prompt reply in the enclosed SASE.

Sincerely,

Joe Writer

If you hear nothing back a month or so after sending such an inquiry, it is appropriate to then send a letter withdrawing the submission. Simply state in your letter, "Since I have not heard back from you on the status of "Achoo" I am withdrawing the manuscript from consideration at *Children's Health*."

If this happens, you have a right to be upset. The publisher has wasted a lot of your time by failing to respond in a timely manner, if at all, to your submission. Editors should have the courtesy to respond if you have included a SASE. But some editors are unprofessional and irresponsible, and in some cases other events beyond your control have transpired—an editor leaves the publication and the new editor does not follow up on her predecessor's correspondence, or a magazine goes out of business altogether. All you can do is learn from the experience and make a note not to submit to that market again. Fortunately, most editors do respond to queries and manuscript submissions within the time frame specified in their guidelines, so don't be discouraged by the few who do not.

When the long-awaited response does come, naturally you want it to be an acceptance rather than a rejection. But either way, you have things to do after that response arrives. Chapter 13 discusses the ins and outs of contracts and other aspects of an acceptance, and Chapter 14 talks about picking up the pieces and moving on after a rejection.

Chapter 13
Contract Considerations & Relevant Rights

The day an acceptance arrives by email, snail mail, or phone is a happy day for a writer, especially when it's the first sale. Even after many acceptances, the thrill persists. Not only does an acceptance mean a paycheck, but it is also an affirmation of a writer's competence.

13.1 Legal Considerations and Contracts

When an editor wishes to buy or assign an article, he will typically offer a contract which specifies rights being purchased, compensation amount, date of publication, deadline for submission or revisions of an assignment, and other details. The writer must wade through the legal language, which is generally not too complex, and should then ask any questions about anything that is unclear before signing the contract. Most aspects of a contract are standard policies for a particular publication and are not open to negotiation. But sometimes, an editor may be willing to negotiate on certain items, such as rights being sold, if the writer asks and has a good reason for doing so. For example, sometimes a publisher that buys all rights may agree to allow the writer to retain book rights if she wishes to later include the article in a book. Some writers also try to negotiate a higher payment, but this is rarely agreed to.

Most assignment contracts that offer payment on publication will specify a "kill fee" to be paid in case the editors decide not to publish the article for reasons beyond the writer's control (such as a lack of space or if the publication folds). If an assignment contract does not mention a kill fee, it is a good idea to ask about this and to insist that one be included. But remember that a kill fee does not apply if an article is not accepted because the writer fails to submit a satisfactory manuscript by the stated deadline. The magazine owes nothing to a writer who fails to live up to the terms of the contract.

If the contract meets with your approval, sign it and return it to the editor by snail mail. (Email is not acceptable for legal documents.)

13.2 Avoid Getting Burned

Reputable publishers uphold their end of a contract, but rarely, you may unknowingly enter into a contract with a fly-by-night operation that runs out of funds, never actually publishes anything, or folds and vanishes from sight. In such cases, you can sue for money owed, but you stand little chance of recovering anything from a defunct or bankrupt organization. The best you can usually do is to report the magazine or Ezine to writer's organizations and publications that can pass the information along to other writers.

I have never had this unfortunate experience, but know that it happens regularly, and it is not something any writer wants to go through. It can happen to anyone, but there are things you can do to minimize the risk of getting burned by a disreputable or unsuccessful publication. First of all, try to submit your work to established magazines with a proven track record. This does not mean that all new, or startup, publications are not legitimate and that they won't be successful and enduring; some do very well. But many startups end up failing in a competitive market. Be particularly wary of new Ezines or other online publication venues that tend to appear and vanish like bad dreams. It's easy for anyone to put up a Website and take it down the next day. Before submitting to a new venture, find out about who the editor is. Do some research about whether he or she was previously associated with established publications, or whether the individual has no track record in publishing. For example, one very successful, high-quality online publication that has only been around for a couple of years is *Imagination Café*. Many writers (and readers) love this market, and a little investigation reveals that its editor, Rosanne Tolin (who was kind enough to allow me to interview her for this book), has been an editor for magazines like *Guideposts for Kids*, newspapers, and Websites for fifteen years. Her solid background as an editor has no doubt played a big role in helping her turn *Imagination Café* into a successful enterprise, and knowing this should definitely bear on a personal decision to submit to this market. While any publication can fall by the wayside any time, it is far less likely to happen if the editor is established in the field. I have read about many startups that list an editor with no publishing background, who happens to be a bored housewife who felt like starting up a magazine one day, and I would not consider sending my work to any such publication.

It's also helpful to look at who the parent company of a new online or print magazine is, if it is not an independent venture. If *Time* magazine or *Sports Illustrated* or *National Geographic* launches a new children's magazine, chances are very good that the new publication will honor its contractual obligations. This is not always true, of course—the great recession has proven that even seemingly rock solid companies can go bankrupt, but it is less likely to happen to companies with longevity and staying power.

You can also find out about a new publication in established writer's forums and newsletters, such as *The Children's Writer*. That is one reason why it's a good idea to subscribe to such newsletters or professional publications—they keep subscribers apprised of other writers' complaints about dubious or disreputable editors or publishers, whether these are new or established enterprises.

Whether you are dealing with a new or established market, keep in mind that sometimes mistakes occur, and an invoice can fall through the cracks and get lost. If you do not get paid when the contract specifies you will be paid, a polite email or phone call to the editor is usually all that's needed to get the oversight corrected. I've only had this happen once, and when I politely informed the editor that I had not yet received a check a month after the expected date, I received an apology stating that the accounting department was way behind schedule. Shortly after that, I received my check.

13.3 Relevant Rights

In addition to details about compensation, another important element of a publishing contract specifies which rights are being purchased. Here is a summary of the different rights a publisher may buy:

- All rights or all world rights means the publisher can publish your manuscript anywhere, any time, any number of times, in any media form, including online or on a CD. The writer no longer owns any rights to re-sell or reproduce the manuscript, though if you make a photocopy to use for informational purposes such as a clip to enclose with a query letter, this is not an attempt to re-sell the piece, so it's okay. Sometimes a writer can re-negotiate a sale of all rights at a later date and a publisher will agree to return limited rights, such as the right to use the manuscript in a book.

- All world serial rights means the publisher can publish a manuscript in serial publications like newspapers and magazines anywhere in the world. The author retains all other rights.

- First rights gives the publisher the right to publish the manuscript for the first time. After publication, rights revert to the author, who can then sell second or reprint rights. Some contracts specify that the author must wait for a certain length of time after publication to re-sell the article, and some say it cannot be re-sold to a magazine in a competing market.

- First North American serial rights means the publisher may publish a manuscript for the first time in a magazine in North America. The author retains other rights.

- Electronic rights gives the publisher the right to publish the manuscript electronically in any form, including on a Website, on a CDROM, or in an ezine or database.

- Second rights, also called reprint rights, allows a publisher to publish material for the second time, after first rights were already sold to another publisher and the material has already been published.

- One-time rights means a publisher can print a manuscript one time only. This is similar to first or second rights, but with one-time rights, the author can sell additional rights before the material is published.

- When a publisher and author sign a work-for-hire contract, the employer (publisher), rather than the writer, is legally considered to be the author, and the publisher owns all rights to the manuscript. Some writers choose not to enter into a work-for-hire contract for this reason, but many (myself included) who engage in work-for-hire find it to be lucrative enough that not owning any rights does not really matter. Plus, when a writer creates a manuscript specifically for a particular publisher in a work-for-hire agreement, the chances of re-selling it elsewhere would be very slim anyway.

13.4 Copyright Laws

The legal basis for owning and selling rights to a manuscript derives from United States copyright laws, which grant an author legal ownership and the right to sell any original manuscript that is written on paper or as a computer file. According to the United States Copyright Office, "Copyright protection subsists from the time the work is created in fixed form. The copyright in the work of authorship immediately becomes the property of the author who created the work. Only the author or those deriving their rights through the author can rightfully claim copyright."

Since a copyright automatically exists "from the time the work is created in fixed form," it is not necessary to register a manuscript with the United States Copyright Office to protect this copyright. Some writers prefer to register their work anyway, since they want a public record established in case of later copyright infringement suits (the work must be officially registered before a lawsuit can commence). Registering a copyright costs $35-$65, and if a writer does this, he should inform an editor of this fact when a manuscript is accepted for publication. However, most writers do not register copyrights on magazine articles, and there is really no reason to do so because the entire magazine is copyrighted when it is published. Some editors say that a writer who registers the copyright is obviously inexperienced, but this is an individual's choice.

A copyright does not protect titles or ideas—only specific manuscripts. An author can legally transfer the copyright on a manuscript to someone else—a publisher or an heir—and one purpose of a publishing contract is to legally transfer the rights to a publisher.

A copyright on a work created after 1978 lasts for the duration of the author's life plus seventy years.

13.5 Copyright Infringement

If a writer believes someone has infringed on his copyright by plagiarizing, copying, or quoting without permission, he can file a copyright infringement lawsuit. At the same time, a writer must be careful not to plagiarize or otherwise infringe on others' copyrights. Plagiarism is a pretty straightforward offense, but copyright infringement when using quotes from a published source can be confusing.

It is important to obtain written permission from the author or publisher to quote from copyrighted material found in books, articles, or Websites. Material published by the United States government is not copyrighted, so this does not apply, but the quote must still be correctly attributed to the source. Any work published in the United States prior to 1923 is also not copyrighted, so no permission to quote is needed, but, again, the source should be acknowledged.

For non-government sources and for material published after 1923, a writer can be sued for copyright infringement if he does not obtain permission to use a quote. There is a great deal of controversy and confusion among writers and legal authorities about what constitutes this type of copyright infringement. The "fair use" doctrine of Title 17 of the U.S. Copyright statute states that it is legal to quote "limited portions" of a copyrighted work in commentary, news reporting, criticism, scholarly reports, educational settings, or research—without obtaining permission. Some books and articles on writing erroneously state that fair use doctrine permits the use of a quote of up to 50 or 100 words without obtaining permission, but the law actually does not specify any such word limits.

Court rulings on whether the fair use doctrine covers certain cases of alleged copyright infringement have been mixed and depend largely on the circumstances. In most cases, if a quote is used for educational and non-profit purposes, such as teaching in a classroom, fair use applies. But when a writer quotes another author in an article that the writer plans to sell, even if it is an educational article, it is open to interpretation whether fair use applies, because the article becomes a commercial or profitable endeavor. Most of the time, no one is going to sue a writer for quoting a couple of sentences and correctly attributing the quote to the rightful source, but the author or publisher could sue if they wanted to. I am certainly not an expert on copyright law or on any other legal aspects of using quotes, but after studying the relevant laws, I would say that it's best to obtain written permission to use a quote from a copyrighted source.

You can get permission to quote by contacting a publisher's permissions department and explaining how and where you intend to use the quote. Sometimes, whoever owns the rights to the material will charge a fee for granting permission, and in such cases a writer must decide whether or not it is worth it to pay the fee or to forget about using the quote. If a publication does not have a permissions department, contact the media relations department or an editor to find out what to do. If the publication has only purchased first or one-time rights from the author of the quote, the author may own the rights to grant permission to quote, so it may be necessary to contact the author directly.

13.6 Everyone's Favorite Topic—Taxes

Slightly off-topic, but relevant to the business aspects of writing, is income taxes. I mention taxes here because they relate to contracts and compensation. A freelance writer is an independent contractor, and as such must pay taxes on earnings. Whether you do your own taxes or hire a professional to do them, it is important to keep track of all payments received and of all business-related expenses that can be used as tax deductions. Owning a business also means being liable for paying a self-employment tax.

If you earn over $600 in a given year from a particular publisher, their accounting department will send you (and the IRS) a 1099 form that must be filed with your tax return. Other earnings should also be documented in the business income section.

If you designate a room in your house as an office used exclusively for your writing business (a desk in the family room doesn't count), you may be entitled to deduct a portion of all your household expenses, including utilities, mortgage, rent, insurance, and others. Keep receipts for all of these, plus for all office supplies, computer-related expenses, money spent for postage, Internet service, mileage traveled to and from interviews and trips to do research in libraries or other places, professional subscriptions, writer's conferences, and other business-related expenses.

Since an independent contractor is not subject to backup withholding, consult a tax expert or the IRS about whether you should be making quarterly estimated federal and state tax payments to avoid non-withholding penalties.

13.7 After the Sale

After you have signed a contract and received payment, don't think of this as the end of your relationship with that editor and publisher. If the experience has been positive and rewarding for both you and the editor, working together in the future can be mutually beneficial, and repeat business is certainly a great career-builder for a freelancer. Mark Haverstock offers some advice on how a writer can do her part to keep windows of opportunity for future collaboration open: "Once you've sold a piece, be sure to approach the editor with a few more of your best ideas over the next year or so. We all want regular work, and editors are looking for regulars they can count on for future articles."

Not every overture you make will be favorably received, just like every query or submission you make to other editors will not result in a sale. But only by continuing to target and submit quality work and ideas will you build a successful business.

Chapter 14
Rejection Resilience

Naturally, writers hate it when they receive a rejection instead of an acceptance. But every writer, even experienced and successful ones, get rejections, and while knowing this is little comfort when you are smarting from the sting, realizing that rejections are a universal part of being a writer at least lets you know that you are not alone.

14.1 Reacting to Rejections

Having past sales does reduce the sting somewhat, since the track record affirms a writer's competence and offers hope that future sales are ahead. But even successful writers are not immune to the frustration and self-doubt that rejections bring. Successful freelancer Jan Fields has this to say about rejections: "Rejections are *horrible*. I get so depressed, really. And I get more rejections now than I did when I was first starting out because I'm trying more risky sales now. For me, rejection is very derailing. I tend to go into at least a 24-hour funk and sometimes longer if the sale was really important to me. Usually, I just have to force myself back in the saddle, back in the writing chair. And it's force. Sometimes making myself write directly after a rejection is like herding cats because my creative side resists the chance of more rejection."

I tend to shrug off rejections without letting them affect my current work, but everyone is different. I have learned to step back and say, "Okay, now I have to decide whether this rejected manuscript is worth sending to the next publication on my list, or whether it really needs some work." I look over the story, make my decision, and move forward. It's not that I don't care about rejections—I really do care, and they really do sting. But a lifetime of developing strategies for dealing with the many challenges that life offers has given me the perspective to rate unfortunate and disappointing things on a relative scale. Compared to many of the things I've been through, getting a rejection is neither tragic nor grounds for giving up. So I treat rejections as important, but not earth-shattering.

For writers who have yet to be published, rejections can be especially discouraging, because they lead to doubts about the individual's fitness as a writer. But keep in mind that most writers do not sell the first manuscript they send out, and sometimes it takes awhile to make that first sale. I sold the first article I submitted because I wrote about something that interested me (acupuncture) and sent it to a children's magazine that focused on health (*Medical Detective*, one of the Children's Better Health Institute publications that is no longer being published) and that happened to find the article well-written and perfect for their readers. But soon after making this sale, I realized that I was certainly not going to avoid the many rejections that all writers receive. I have collected scores and scores of rejections over the years, sometimes because I didn't do enough homework on the publication to which I was submitting, and sometimes for unknown reasons. I received fourteen rejections on one article before selling it to *Cricket*. I have one children's picture book manuscript that I have been submitting for twenty years (really!). I've gotten quite a few positive comments about it from editors, but no acceptance, and I've revised it about six times. I think it's a good story, and I'm going to continue to try to sell it.

It takes different lengths of time for different writers to make that first sale. Suzanne Lieurance, who started writing professionally in the 1970's, did not make her first sale for a year after she made her first submission. It took Anne Renaud eight years to make a sale—she initially tried to sell children's books, and received many rejections, but began selling her work when she switched to writing children's magazine articles. It only took Mark Haverstock about two months to make his first sale, and Fiona Bayrock sold the very first article she submitted, so rejection histories vary widely.

Some aspiring writers never get published because they give up after a few or a lot of rejections. But quitting is a sure-fire way to not succeed. Writer Richard Bach once said, "A professional writer is an amateur who didn't quit." If you don't keep submitting after a rejection, you can't get published. I always think of a line from the book and movie *Chariots of Fire*, which happens to be one of my favorites, when I find myself getting discouraged about rejections. In *Chariots of Fire*, British Olympic runner Harold Abrahams became discouraged about losing a race and said to his girlfriend, "If I can't win, I won't run." His girlfriend, actress Sybil Gordon, replied, "If you don't run, you can't win."

There are ways of looking at rejections that can help writers find the will to persevere. But before I discuss these strategies, I will describe the different types of rejections in the next section.

14.2 Types of Rejection Letters

Most rejection letters are form letters that say something like "Thank you for your submission. We regret to inform you that it does not meet our editorial needs, and wish you the best of luck in placing it elsewhere." This type of rejection can mean that the topic is wrong, the timing is wrong because a similar piece was recently published or is scheduled to be published in the future, the publication is entirely inappropriate for the manuscript, or the manuscript is not any good. The phrase "does not meet our editorial needs" is very frustrating because it tells you absolutely nothing about the reason for the rejection.

If you receive a form letter like this, read over the manuscript with a critical eye to see if there is room for improvement, and if so, make some revisions. Re-evaluate whether your market research was thorough, and ask yourself if the research sources you used were reliable. If you can't find anything wrong, then send the piece off to another publication.

Some publishers' form letters contain a checklist an editor can use to let a writer know why the manuscript is being rejected, and this is much more helpful than the "does not meet our editorial needs" line is. If an editor uses a checklist to inform you that the magazine recently published or is going to publish a similar article, you can be relieved that your timing was just off and that there is probably nothing wrong with the manuscript (unless the editor didn't even read the submission and failed to mention this). But if the editor checked a box indicating that your submission was inappropriate for the publication or did not follow the writer's guidelines, this tells you that you need to do more careful market research in the future.

Editor Debra Hess says *Highlights* rejects many manuscripts because "The most common mistake that writers make is to not consult our guidelines. Articles that are submitted without a bibliography are immediately returned, as are submissions that are over the word limit. These submissions are not even read. Of course, a writer is free to resubmit the same article with the appropriate backup."

If the stated reason on a checklist was something along the lines of saying that the piece was not well-written or that the sources used were unacceptable, you can learn from this feedback too. Go back and review the types of sources that are preferred by the publication. Analyze what is wrong with your grammar, word choices, beginning, middle, or ending, and do some editing and rewriting—but don't resubmit to the same publication after editing, unless the editor specifically asked you to do so. Always keep in mind that no matter what the reason for a rejection is, the rejection is final unless the editor says otherwise. It is not acceptable to argue with an editor about her decision, even if it seems arbitrary and wrong to you. Arguing by mail, email, or phone will get you nowhere; in fact editors will not take such calls or respond to such mail, and will probably vow not to consider your submissions in the future.

While no editor will engage in an argument about the finality of a rejection, some may be glad to entertain questions about why a query or manuscript was rejected. But be aware that most editors are too busy to do this, so don't be surprised if your questions are ignored. Brad Riddell of *Boys' Life*, however, is one editor who will respond to such questions. "If you get rejected, don't be afraid to ask how to better the query or hone ideas in the future. And then try again. Know the publication you're querying and be persistent," he says.

Many writers become frustrated by form rejection letters, even those that include a checklist, because they are impersonal and often not detailed enough to be helpful. But remember that editors get hundreds or even thousands of submissions each year, and they do not have time to write a personalized rejection notice for every manuscript they reject. Editors do far more than just reading manuscripts. They plan future magazine issues, do layouts, coordinate illustrations and photos, edit material they purchase, and many other things. So try to understand the reason for form rejection letters.

14.3 Good Rejections

When an editor does take the time to write a personalized note, it usually means that he liked the submission enough to comment on the reasons for the rejection or that he is willing to reconsider it if the author makes some changes. I call personalized rejection letters "good rejections." I find these rejections encouraging because they show me that the editor thought enough of my work to let me know why she was rejecting it, or better still, that the door is still open if I make some changes.

If an editor asks for revisions that seem reasonable, there is no reason not to revise away, even though this does not guarantee an acceptance. Most of the time, an editor who requests revisions offers some guidance about what those revisions should entail, and this can be very helpful. But don't be in a big hurry to finish the edits and send the manuscript back right away. It may take a week or two weeks or more to clarify facts, add requested information, or make other changes, and it's important not to do a quick, sloppy job. Give yourself enough time to think about whether your revised version satisfies the editor's requests before sending it in.

Sometimes an editor will mention in a personalized rejection letter that he likes your writing, but regrets that he cannot accept a manuscript because of space limitations or subject matter or whatever. He may invite you to submit other material in the future, and of course this is a great opportunity to keep in mind for future submissions. If you do send something else, be sure to mention the invitation in your cover letter. But don't be tempted to send off something right away just to strike while you are fresh in the editor's mind. First, be sure that the other article is appropriate and well-written—or it may receive a form rejection letter. If you don't have anything appropriate on hand, file the editor's letter in your idea or publisher information folder and keep it in mind when you decide to write on a new topic that can be slanted toward that publication. I always save personalized rejection letters for future reference and encouragement—but I never save form letters. Some writers do save them, but I think it would be a waste of valuable space, since I've gotten so many!

Sometimes a "good" rejection can lead to an assignment as well as to a lead on a future submission. My assignment and contract to write this Treasure Trove book came out of a rejected picture book submission I sent to E & E Publishing, which publishes children's picture books as well as adult books about writing. The editor noticed that I stated in my cover letter that I had published hundreds of magazine articles. At the time, she was contemplating publishing a how-to book on writing and selling children's magazine articles, and she asked me if I would be interested in writing it. I replied that I would be very interested, and after I sent some samples of my work and after we traded emails about what the book would involve, I got the assignment. So even rejections can have happy endings.

14.4 Rejection Resilience

But these happy endings won't happen to writers who give up and stop submitting, and changing the way you view rejections can help keep you motivated to keep trying. It helps if you view rejections in a business-like manner and realize that they are not a personal slap in the face or omens that you are not meant to be a professional writer. A rejection is a business decision by a particular editor. It is a statement of the fact that your query or manuscript was not right for this editor at this time. The reason for the decision may be that the story did not appeal to this editor (everyone, including editors, has personal tastes, passions, and dislikes). Or the reason may be that the timing was off or that the manuscript needs work. But the rejection is a statement about the manuscript, not about you. If the piece needs work, fix it. If the timing was bad, send it elsewhere. But don't think of the rejection as an indication that you lack what it takes to be a successful writer!

Jan Fields shares how she overcomes the sting of a rejection and moves on: "Ultimately, I keep in mind that rejection is about the product I produced. For some reason, unrelated to *me personally*, that product did not work for that specific place. It's not really about me or my work overall. I have plenty of proof—decades of proof—that I can write for publication. So I have to keep telling myself the truth that way and to remember, I only really fail at this if I quit. I will sell again. It's inevitable. Of course, I'll also be rejected again... but during those gloomy days of needing up-talk, I try not to remember that part." Even unpublished writers who do not have a publishing history to fall back on can benefit from recognizing that rejections are judgments about manuscripts, not people.

Fiona Bayrock echoes the need to persevere and learn from rejections. "Don't give up too soon. Perseverance is really important in this business. It's a matter of getting the right idea on the right editor's desk at the right time. That's a challenge, even for those of us who have been doing this for a while. If you've been rejected by the same editor several times, make sure you're aiming for the right place. By that I mean make sure you know the magazine well so you're pitching ideas that interest the magazine's readers and are in keeping with what the magazine usually contains," she says.

Suzanne Lieurance, who teaches writing, emphasizes that putting the spotlight on learning, rather than on any hurt feelings that a rejection brings, is essential for dealing successfully with rejections. "I always tell my coaching clients to focus on the writing itself and publication will naturally follow. You have to submit to be rejected, so rejection is just part of the process of becoming a successful, widely published writer. But, as rejections come in, just continue studying and practicing your writing and your writing will keep improving."

Christine Venzon finds that continuing to write about things that interest her helps her deal with rejections because she is doing something she enjoys. She advises, "Write about something you love. It's more fun, and that's important, because this job is too hard and rejection is too common to have to stomach not liking what you're writing about on top of it all. Plus it helps you build your platform, as they like to say, all those things that make you salable and an authority. Say you like crafts. You can give lessons at libraries, get involved in craft guilds, all things to beef up your credentials. If you don't like crafts but try to write about them, you're not going to do that stuff, and it'll hurt your chances of making a sale, because you're competing against people who really enjoy them."

Pulling It All Together

A willingness to keep learning from every outcome of the writing and marketing process —including rejections and publication triumphs—is essential for short- and long-term success as a writer. With perseverance, a genuine love of writing, and the dedication to master the principles you have learned about in this book, a successful career in writing children's magazine articles may be closer at hand than you ever dreamed. So good luck—and get busy!

Appendix A
Grammar Gateway

The thought of spending time with rules of grammar may be enough to send many people screaming for an exit, but before you begin writing articles, it's important to go over some basic rules and common stumbling blocks. Even experienced writers sometimes have trouble with proper grammar and spelling, and editors do not look kindly on these types of mistakes. Poor grammar indicates that a writer is sloppy and does not pay attention to details, and such transgressions lead to rejections.

This appendix will go over some common grammatical errors and causes for confusion. It is in no way intended to be a comprehensive guide; the topics of proper English grammar and usage take up entire books by themselves!

A.1 Parts of Speech

Keep in mind that the main purpose of proper grammar is to convey ideas clearly and unambiguously. To achieve this goal, you must use words, sentences, and punctuation correctly. There are a great many rules and exceptions to the rules of grammar and spelling, so mastering them can get a little tricky. I will begin by going over the basic parts of speech and common errors that involve these words.

A.1.1 Nouns and Pronouns

Nouns are words that name someone, something, or an abstract idea. Woman, book, garden, family, intelligence, and strength are all nouns. Proper nouns name particular people, animals, or places, and are always capitalized. Examples of proper nouns are Jasper, Mrs. Jones, New York, and The Metropolitan Opera. Pronouns are words that replace nouns. Common pronouns are me, you, his, ours, somebody, herself, and anyone.

Nouns and pronouns can be made plural, and they can serve as either the subject or object of a phrase or sentence. The subject does whatever is being done, and the object is acted upon. In "Billy rode his bike," Billy is the subject and bike is the object. By changing the words' order, the subject can become the object, and vice-versa: "The bike was ridden by Billy."

Most errors involving nouns and pronouns arise from making them plural or from failing to correctly link nouns with the pronouns that replace them. Most nouns are made plural by adding s to the end of the word. But in some compound words, the s should be added after the first part of the word, as in the plural of brother-in-law being brothers-in-law and the plural of commander-in-chief being commanders-in-chief.

Nouns ending in ch, sh, s, x, z, or z are made plural by adding es. If a noun ends in y, change the y to an i before adding es if the y is preceded by a consonant – city becomes cities, berry becomes berries. But if the y is preceded by a vowel, simply add s – key becomes keys, toy becomes toys. In some words that end in f, such as leaf and half, change the f to a v before adding es. In wife and life, change the f to a v and add s to make a plural.

Atypical plurals that are not made by adding s or es also cause confusion. Examples are alumnus (plural is alumni), appendix (appendices), bacterium (bacteria), criterion (criteria), datum (data), focus (foci), hypothesis (hypotheses), index (indices), larva (larvae), memorandum (memoranda), phenomenon (phenomena), stimulus (stimuli), vertebra (vertebrae), child (children), man (men), woman (women), and tooth (teeth). Some atypical plurals are the same word as the singular: deer, bison, moose, scissors, series, sheep, species, and swine.

One common noun/pronoun-related error occurs when a pronoun fails to agree in number with the noun it represents. This noun is known as the antecedent. In "A dog is a wonderful companion, but it requires a lot of care," "dog" is the antecedent and "it" is the pronoun. Many people mistakenly write "A dog is a wonderful companion, but they require a lot of care." This is wrong because the antecedent is singular and the pronoun is plural. Another example of this is "Each person must do their share of the work." Each is singular, and their is plural, so this is wrong. The correct sentence would be "Each person must do his share of the work." If a pronoun follows two antecedents, it should agree in number with the closest antecedent. In "The boy and his sisters lost their way," the pronoun "their" is correct because it agrees in number with sisters.

It's also important not to switch from using a first or second person pronoun to using a third person pronoun in a sentence. First person pronouns include I, me, my, our, and we. Second person pronouns include you and your. Third person pronouns include it, this, that, he, she, one, him, her, they, their, and them. The sentence "You can succeed if one tries hard enough" is incorrect because "you" is a second person pronoun and "one" is a third person pronoun. The correct sentence would be "You can succeed if you try hard enough."

The pronouns who, whoever, whom, and whomever also cause much confusion. Use who and whoever when the pronoun is the subject of the verb, as in "It was Jared who fell down" or "Whoever wants to come along may do so." Use whom or whomever when the pronoun is the object of the verb, as in "He told his story to whomever would listen" or "Ask not for whom the bell tolls."

One more important pronoun rule is to avoid using indefinite pronouns, such as "you" and "they," that do not refer to a noun. In "They say cigarettes cause cancer," the pronoun "they" does not refer to anyone in particular, so it should not be used. Instead, write "Doctors say cigarettes cause cancer." The sentence "You get sick from smoking" is incorrect for the same reason. Write "People get sick from smoking" instead. Note that addressing the reader directly, as in "Do you know where a bat sleeps?" is a completely different usage of the pronoun "you" and is grammatically fine.

A.1.2 Adventures in Adjectives

Adjectives modify or describe nouns or pronouns, never verbs or other adjectives. Sometimes nouns or pronouns themselves can be used as adjectives, as in "He gave a present to his boss," where the pronoun "his" serves as the adjective. Clauses and phrases, as well as single words, can serve as adjectives. A clause is a group of words that contain a subject, or noun, and a verb. A phrase is a group of words that does not contain both a noun and a verb.

Adjective words, clauses, or phrases may precede or follow the word they modify. In "Lettuce is green," the adjective "green" follows the noun "lettuce." But many errors and ambiguities arise when adjectives are not placed correctly. "The charging lion only gave us three seconds to escape" is incorrect because the adjective "only" is supposed to modify the noun phrase "three seconds," not the verb "gave." The correct sentence would read "The charging lion gave us only three seconds to escape."

Be careful not to leave out adjectives that are needed to clarify the meaning of a sentence as well. In "She gave presents to her boss and mentor," it is not clear whether the boss and mentor are one person or two. Adding the adjectives "both" and another "her" would clear this up: "She gave presents to both her boss and her mentor." If the boss and mentor is the same person, "She gave presents to the man who was both her boss and mentor" would clarify this.

Another stumbling block is the adjectives "a" and "an," which are known as articles. Use "a" before nouns that begin with a consonant and "an" before nouns that begin with a vowel or a silent "h." For example, an heirloom or an hour are silent "h" words that are correctly preceded by "an."

A.1.3 Vexatious Verbs

Verbs are action or state of being words. Verbs can be finite or nonfinite. Finite verbs can stand on their own and form complete predicates. Predicates are verbs or verb phrases that explain what the subject of the sentence is doing, as in speak, run, or do. A nonfinite verb is called a verbal. Verbals cannot stand alone and cannot form complete predicates; thus they must be accompanied by a finite verb to make a complete sentence. There are three types of verbals: infinitives, gerunds, and participles. An infinitive is a verb preceded by "to." It can function as a verb, noun, adjective, or adverb. In "To write using impeccable grammar is my goal," the infinitive "to write" functions as a noun. In "The place to go is on Main Street," the infinitive is an adjective phrase that modifies "place." In "He prepared to talk about his plans," the infinitive functions as an adverb which modifies "prepared."

A gerund is a verb ending in "ing" that is being used as a noun, as in "I like swimming." A participle functions as both a verb and an adjective, as in "The singing bird flew away." Here, the word "singing" is a participle.

Many errors with verbs involve misuse of infinitives, gerunds, and participles. In "She likes to run and playing tennis," the infinitive "to run" is incorrectly combined with the participle "playing." The sentence should read "She likes running and playing tennis" or "She likes to run and to play tennis." The sentence "When traveling abroad, the price should be considered," is incorrect because the gerund phrase "traveling abroad" cannot stand on its own, and needs to refer to a subject. This can be corrected by changing it to "When traveling abroad, one needs to consider the price."

Other common verb errors involve incorrect verb tenses. Verb tenses should remain consistent within a sentence. The sentence "The bear walks into the campsite and trampled the tent" is incorrect because "walks" is present tense and "trampled" is past tense. The correct sentence would be "The bear walked into the campsite and trampled the tent" or "The bear walks into the campsite and tramples the tent."

Verbs must also agree in person and number with their subject. "I likes you" is wrong because "I" is a first person singular pronoun, and "likes" should be used with third person singular pronouns, as in "He likes you." But some nouns appear to be plural, but are actually singular, and in such instances a singular verb should be used. An example is "politics." The sentence "Politics is the lowest form of human interaction" is correct, even though "politics" appears to be plural. Another example is "economics." The sentence "Economics is the study of financial trends" is correct for the same reason.

When a number-noun combination is plural, but is used as a single unit, a singular verb should also be used, as in "Six hours is too long to wait." When two singular nouns are joined by "and," a plural verb is required, as in "Both John and Mary were tired." But two singular nouns joined by "or" or "nor" need a singular verb, as in "Neither John nor Mary was there on time" or "Either the door or the wall needs painting."

A verb must also agree in number with the noun it follows. In "The worst part of losing a game is the coach's lecture and having to congratulate the winners," the singular verb "is" correctly agrees with the singular noun "part." If the sentence were reversed to read "The coach's lecture and having to congratulate the winners are the worst parts of losing a game," the plural verb "are" is correct because it follows two noun phrases (the coach's lecture and having to congratulate the winners).

A.1.4 Adversarial Adverbs

An adverb modifies a verb, adjective, or another adverb, but never a noun or pronoun. In "She walked quickly down the street," the adverb "quickly" modifies the verb "walked." In "Dinner is almost ready," the adverb "almost" modifies the adjective "ready." In "Be sure to respond very quickly," the adverb "very" modifies the adverb "quickly."

Some words can be either adverbs or adjectives, depending on how they are used. In "we left early," "early" is an adverb that modifies "left." In "We got an early start," "early" is an adjective that modifies the noun "start." Other times, adjectives become adverbs by adding "ly" (as in quick and quickly), and people often misuse such adjectives to modify a verb or such adverbs to modify a noun. For example, the sentence "He runs too slow" is incorrect because "slow" is an adjective, and it cannot be used to modify the verb "runs." The correct sentence would use the adverb "slowly." "That's a real good drawing" is incorrect because the adjective "real" cannot modify the adjective "good." The correct sentence uses the adverb really and would read "That's a really good drawing."

Another common error is improperly substituting an adverb for a noun. In "Anemia is where the body has too few red blood cells," the adverb "where" is incorrectly replacing a noun phrase. The correct sentence would be "Anemia is a condition in which the body has too few red blood cells." Many people also improperly use the adverb "when," as in "Hacking is when someone breaks into a computer." The correct sentence would be "Hacking is the act of breaking into a computer."

A.1.5 Confusing Conjunctions

The fact that sometimes adverbs can also be other parts of speech known as conjunctions can cause further confusion. For instance, "when" is a type of conjunction called a conjunctive adverb, since it not only modifies, but also links other words together. The distinction between adverbs and conjunctions, though, is not important as long as the words are used correctly.

Common conjunctions, or linking words, include and, are, but, so, because, for, either, neither, if, since, while, which, and unless. Writers often misuse or overuse these words. Misuses often involve employing the wrong conjunction. In "The crocodile tried to bite the boat and could not reach it," using "but" instead of "and" would be best because it would clarify the meaning. The conjunction "because" is also often misused after the phrases "the reason is" or "the reason was." "The reason I can't go is because I have to work" is incorrect. The correct sentence would be "The reason I can't go is that I have to work" or "I can't go because I have to work"; if you use "because," don't also use "the reason is."

Many people erroneously combine the conjunctions "and" and "which," "but" and "which," "and" and "who," or "but" and "who." In "I have a great recipe, and which you will find easy to follow," the "and" should be deleted. In "She initially felt compassion, but which soon gave way to anger," remove the "but." In "Jim is a hardworking person and who never cheats," the "and" should be deleted.

The conjunctions "that" and "which" tend to be misused as well, but it's often tricky to decide when they are necessary. In "He said that you should return the books that you borrowed," the first "that" should probably stay and the second one should probably be deleted. But in "He believes that antibiotics cause bacteria to mutate," the "that" is necessary to prevent the sentence from sounding like the person believes something the antibiotics said. In "The lion returned to finish off the zebra which it had left in the clearing," the "which" is not necessary. But in "There are many chemicals which can cause cancer," "which" is essential for making a coherent sentence. If in doubt, it's usually helpful to read a sentence aloud. In addition, try to avoid using several "thats" or "whichs" in a sentence or paragraph.

One more issue involving conjunctions concerns beginning a sentence with "and," "so," or "but." Some writing experts say it is not correct to do this, but most agree it's okay to do in moderation. Sometimes starting a sentence with one of these words seems natural. In an article I did about dog heroes, I wrote, "Most dogs live up to their reputation as man's best friend by being caring and loyal companions. But some dogs go beyond the usual dog wonderfulness and do things that classify them as true heroes." Here, beginning the second sentence with "but" seemed natural. So don't fret about occasionally starting a sentence with a conjunction. Just don't overdo it.

A.1.6 Pesky Prepositions

Prepositions are similar to conjunctions, and some are interchangeable. But usually a preposition establishes a relationship between other words, as well as linking them together. Common prepositions are by, before, after, for, since, with, over, off, on, about, of, up, down, near, far, always, until, across, at, between, inside, outside, from, and under. A preposition must be followed by a noun, pronoun, or noun clause; never by a verb unless the verb is being used as an infinitive or gerund. "These shoes are for run" is incorrect, but "These shoes are for running" is correct because "running" is a gerund.

Most errors involving prepositions arise from using too many of them. "He leaped off of the building" is incorrect because the preposition "of" is extraneous. In "Where are you going to?" the "to" is extraneous. In "In this book it discusses about lions," "in," "it," and "about" are all extraneous. The sentence is correct as "This book discusses lions."

Ending a sentence with a preposition is also wrong—most of the time. If in doubt as to whether or not it is acceptable, ask yourself whether rearranging the sentence would be especially awkward. In "This is what I have spent my whole life working for," ending with the preposition "for" is acceptable, since moving the word to the middle of the sentence would be extremely awkward: "This is for what I have spent my whole life working." You could change it to "This is the purpose for which I have spent my whole life working" and have a grammatically correct sentence, but the original sentence ending in "for" is less contrived. Some people, including some editors, insist on never ending a sentence with a preposition, but most are willing to bend the rule if doing so leads to a less contrived construction.

Another sentence that is fine to end with a preposition is "I need someone to lean on," since "I need someone on whom to lean" is very awkward. But "What color paper should I print this on?" is a tossup, because changing it to "On what color paper should I print this?" does not result in a particularly awkward sentence. However, ending the sentence with "on" results in a more conversational tone, so it's probably best left that way in most instances.

A.2 Spelling Challenges

Besides misuse of the parts of speech, spelling mistakes account for a great many of the errors writers make. A computer spell checker will catch most of these mistakes, so I will not go into most of the common spelling errors. But the spell checker will not catch misspellings where a word is spelled correctly in one context but not in another. Words that sound alike but have different meanings (homonyms) are most often involved, so I will give examples of the most common stumbling blocks.

Your, yore, and you're are often confused and thus misspelled in their correct context. "You're" is a contraction for "you are." "Your" is an indication that you own something, as in "your shoes." "Yore" refers to a long time ago, as in "There were no TVs in days of yore." If you write "you're shoes," you are really saying "you are shoes." Its and it's are equally as abused. "It's" is a contraction of "it is." "Its" is a possessive pronoun like "your" is. Thus, if you write "The dog scratched it's head," you are really saying "The dog scratched it is head." They're, their, and there are also widely confused. 'They're" means "they are," "their" is a possessive pronoun, and "there" signifies a direction in which something is going. Correct usage is: "They're going on a trip," "The kittens lost their mittens," and "We are going there on Sunday." In the oft-confused whose and who's, "whose" is a possessive pronoun, as in "Whose jacket is this?" "Who's" is a contraction of "who is," as in "Who's the best cook?"

Here are some more homonyms that are often confused:

- To, too, and two. "To" signifies where someone or something is going, as in "We are headed to the store." "Too" means also or overly, as in "He ate too much" or "John is coming with us too." "Two" is the number after one, as in "She ate two cookies.

- Accept and except. "Except" means to omit, as in "Everyone except Tom left the party." "Accept" means to receive or agree with, as in "I accept your apology."

- Born and borne. "Born" means brought into the world, as in "The baby was born at midnight." "Borne" means carried: "He has borne a great burden."

- Break and brake. "Break" as a verb means to destroy: "That chair will break if you sit on it." "Break" as a noun means luck or misfortune: "He caught a bad break," or can mean an interlude: "He took a five minute break." "Brake" is a noun or verb meaning something that slows or stops, or the act of slowing or stopping: "He applied the brakes."

- Sight, site, and cite. "Sight" means a view: "The oasis was a welcome sight." "Site" means a place: "He drove to the building site." "Cite" means to refer to: "I will cite the journal article in my manuscript."
- Complement and compliment. "Complement" means to complete or enhance: "That hat comple-

ments your suit." "Compliment" means flattery: "He complimented her new dress."

- Creak and creek. A "creak" is a noise: "These floorboards creak." A "creek" is a small stream: "The creek in the back yard has no fish."

- Discreet and discrete. "Discreet" means inconspicuous: "Please be discreet when you investigate this crime." "Discrete" means separate: "She placed the berries in discrete piles."

- Here and hear. "Here" means in a certain place: "I left my wallet right here." "Hear" means to perceive a sound: "I hope I hear my alarm clock."

- Insight and incite. "Insight" means understanding: "She has great insight into her problems." "Incite" means to provoke: "That Internet posting will incite anger."

- Led and lead. "Led" is the past tense of the verb "lead": "He led her across the street." "Lead" as a noun is a heavy metal: "This paint contains lead."

- Miner and minor. A "miner" is someone who works in a mine: "The miner got stuck underground." "Minor" means inconsequential or refers to a person under legal age: "It is illegal to serve liquor to a minor" or "He has some minor injuries."
- Pare, pair, and pear. To "pare" means to trim; "I have to pare the potatoes." A "pair" is two of a kind:

"I bought a pair of shoes." A "pear" is a type of fruit: "The pear was not ripe."

- Past and passed. "Past" means what came before: "Her past haunts her." "Passed" is the past tense of the verb "to pass": "The car passed us on the right."

- Prey and pray. "Prey" can be a noun or verb referring to the victim of a predator: "The lion stalked its prey" or "Lions prey on zebras." To "pray" is to entreat or worship: "Please pray for healing."

- Principal and principle. A "principal" refers to a person in charge or a sum of money: "The school principal can be strict" or "He paid down the principal on his loan." A "principle" is a doctrine: "Stealing is against my principles."

- Than and then. "Than" is a conjunction used to compare two things: "The new one works better than the old one did." "Then" expresses when something is happening: "He then completed the job."

- Vial and vile. A "vial" is a small container: "She bought a vial of perfume." "Vile" means repulsive: "His language is vile."

- Waive and wave. To "waive" means to give up: "He waived his right to a trial." As a noun, a "wave" is a swell or crest: "The surfer rode a wave." As a verb, "wave" means to move something back and forth: "She waved her arms."

- Weather and whether. As a noun, "weather" signifies atmospheric conditions: "There's some bad weather ahead." As a verb, "weather" means to endure: "He has weathered some intense storms." "Whether" is a conjunction that refers to an alternative: "He can't decide whether to stay or to leave."

A.3 Sentence Structure

Words, of course, must be combined into sentences to write a manuscript, and there are grammatical rules that govern sentence structure and clarity. A sentence is a group of words that contain a complete thought. It must contain a subject and a predicate to be complete. Many errors occur when an incomplete fragment replaces a sentence. The fragment "when he suddenly appeared" does not contain a complete thought or action, so it is not a sentence. However, sometimes a fragment is acceptable if a subject or predicate is implied by the context. In Jane asked, "How often do you jog?" and Joan replied, "Twice a week," the fragment "Twice a week" is acceptable because it implies "I jog twice a week" in this context.

Other times, a sentence fragment used for emphasis is acceptable, as in "He wasn't about to give up. Not this time." However, some writers tend to overuse fragments for emphasis, and, like other stylistic quirks, moderation is key. In "The purring stopped. For a minute. Then it restarted. Loudly. Like an engine. For the next hour," there are probably too many emphatic fragments, in my opinion. But not all writers and editors would agree on this; I've actually seen this type of thing published.

Run-on sentences that contain more than one unified thought are another common error. The sentence "Scientists do not understand why drug therapy works only fifty percent of the time they have begun to uncover some clues" is obviously a run-on. Length, however, has little to do with whether or not a sentence is a run-on. "The dog ate dinner fell asleep quickly" is also a run-on. Run-ons can be corrected by making two sentences or by using a conjunction or a semicolon to join two related thoughts. "The dog ate dinner, then fell asleep quickly" uses a conjunction to form one acceptable sentence. "Scientists do not understand why drug therapy works only fifty percent of the time; they have, however, begun to uncover some clues" uses a semicolon and the conjunction "however" to turn a run-on into an acceptable sentence.

Other common sentence errors involve lack of clarity. Be sure explanatory clauses follow the word they are explaining. If you write "He brought the food to the table that had been in the refrigerator" it sounds like the table had been in the refrigerator. The clause "that had been in the refrigerator" should follow the word "food." In "His leg hurt when he went to the hospital," it is unclear whether he went to the hospital because his leg hurt or if the leg started hurting when he went to the hospital. Change it to "He went to the hospital because his leg hurt badly" for clarification. In "While driving home, the brakes failed," it seems like the brakes were driving the car. "The brakes failed while I was driving home" or "While I was driving home, the brakes failed" clarifies this. Using the first sentence if the next sentence is about home and the second if the next sentence is about brakes is best.

A.4 Punctuation Pointers

Many times, using correct punctuation can help clarify the intended meaning of a sentence, and may even preclude the need to change around wording. In fact, the primary purpose of punctuation marks is to clarify the meaning and relationships between words in a sentence, as well as to end, enclose, or separate these words.

Periods, which are most often used to end a sentence, are not usually troublesome. Periods are also used after an abbreviation, as in Mrs. Smith; or before a decimal or number of cents, as in .05 or $3.45. Use three periods (called ellipsis periods) to indicate an omission from a quote or sentence. For example, "This new discovery changes our thinking about dinosaurs... we now believe some mothers stayed with their babies." Some writers use ellipsis periods to indicate that something more happened, without saying what it is, as in "The tiger disappeared into the jungle..."

A.4.1 Parentheses and Brackets

Use parentheses to enclose a brief explanation within a sentence, as in "Kangaroos are the largest marsupials (animals with a pouch) in Australia." Use one or two parentheses to number a sequence: 1) or (1) turn left on Main Street 2) go two miles 3) turn left on Elm. Use brackets to enclose words you are adding to a direct quote to clarify its meaning, as in Dr. John Smith states, "Many conventional [Western] medical doctors now recommend acupuncture."

A.4.2 Confusing Commas

Commas can be confusing and troublesome. They are used in several ways:

- Commas separate a list or series of words: He bought apples, oranges, and pears at the store.

- When elements is a series contain commas, use a semicolon to separate major categories: He bought crisp, red apples; green, red, and black grapes; and three mangoes.

- Commas can introduce or separate phrases: I'm asking you again, where do you want to eat dinner?

- Commas can add clarity: Once inside, the child stopped trembling.

- Do not use a comma when the subject of two clauses or phrases is the same: He walked quickly and arrived home ten minutes later.

- Do not use a comma to separate a subject and its verb or a verb and its object: The man standing there is Joe Post. (Do not use a comma after "there"). Swimming in that area is dangerous. (Do not use a comma after "area").

- A comma can introduce or end a direct quote: He said, "I'm leaving." "Don't worry about it," she said.

- Do not use a comma before an indirect quote: Paul told me he was getting a new job. (Don't be tempted to put a comma after "me").

- A comma is used after a salutation in an informal letter: Dear Joe,

- Do not use a comma after the conjunctions "but" or "and": It would be wrong to write "But, I was wrong."

- Do not use a comma to replace a necessary word: "The team worked together, won the game" is incorrect. The sentence needs the preposition "and" instead of a comma: "The team worked together and won the game."

- Use a comma to separate numbers containing four or more digits: 2,300 or $151,240.

- Use commas to enclose dates, places, titles, or initials: He arrived on October 6, 2010, in New York. Atlanta, Georgia, is not a typical Southern town. Carl Jones, M.D., and his wife, Linda Jones, PhD, arrived next.

- Use commas to enclose qualifying or parenthetical phrases and appositives: The girl, however, knew he was lying. Whales, on the other hand, are mammals. This chapter, tedious though it may seem, contains important information for writers.
- Use commas to enclose a name or pronoun being directly addressed: You, my friend, are crazy. You are wild and silly, John, but I still like you.

A.4.3 Colons and Semicolons

A colon is primarily used to introduce a list or quotation after an introductory statement which reveals that something is about to follow, as in "Jack values three things in life: family, church, and football" or in "The senator then stated: 'I am the most corrupt politician in the country.'" However, do not use a colon when a preposition, verb, or conjunction follows the introductory phrase, as in these cases, where the verb "are" follows these phrases: "The most widely eaten foods are rice, beans, and milk" or "The three things Jack values most in life are family, church, and football."

Also use a colon after a salutation in a formal letter, as in Dear Mr. Jones: or to separate the title and subtitle of a book, as in *Vanishing Wildlife: A Guide to Endangered Species,* and between the hour and minute in writing the time, as in 2:35 PM.

A semicolon primarily coordinates parts of a sentence, indicates a longer pause than a comma does, or separates elements of a series that already contains commas. An example of using a semicolon to coordinate sentence clauses that are not joined by a conjunction is "Don't think of leaving yet; you've barely eaten anything." Such a sentence could be made into two sentences, but a semicolon unifies the clauses into one coherent sentence. A semicolon can also be used to separate clauses that are joined by a conjunctive adverb such as besides, however, nonetheless, nevertheless, therefore, thus, hence, consequently, or furthermore. "The mechanic could not diagnose the problem; thus, we had to take the car to another garage."

A.4.4 Hyphens and Dashes

Hyphens and dashes can be very confusing. It is often difficult to determine whether or not to insert a hyphen between two words, to join the two words into a compound word, or to leave them as two discrete words. Hyphens are generally used in the following situations:

- When two adjectives or an adjective-adverb or adjective-noun combination modifies a noun as a unit, as in absent-minded professor, fast-moving car, good-natured fellow, long-needed break, or first-rate manuscript. However, when two independent adverbs or adjectives modify a noun or verb, no hyphen should be used, as in "The dog has pale yellow fur."

- Sometimes adjective phrases that preceded a noun are hyphenated when they are used as a unit, as in on-the-job training, a matter-of-fact attitude, and the five-to-eight-year-old age group.

- Between parts of compound nouns, as in sister-in-law and Jack-of-all-trades. With some compound nouns, using a hyphen or combining the two parts into one word is optional, and may depend on editorial preference. For example, both farfetched and far-fetched are correct, state-wide and statewide are correct, and trademark and trade-mark are correct.

- Between parts of compound numbers: forty-five and ninety-eight.

- When a prefix like un, anti, pro, or pre is used with a proper noun or a numeral, as in pro-American, non-Catholic, or pre-2001.

- To distinguish a homonym, as in "I need to re-cover this book." Otherwise, the meaning would be unclear.

- Indicates a range, as in "Read pages 3-5" or "The great recession lasted from 2007-2025."

A dash looks like an elongated hyphen, but is used differently. A dash:

- Indicates an interruption or shift in thought. Sometimes a dash is used instead of a comma or parentheses for emphasis. In "I've been wondering—actually obsessing over—whether my best option is quitting my job," the dashes indicate emphasis and a shift in thought. In "White blood cells—also known as leukocytes—fight infections," the dashes are used as a shift in thought instead of commas or parentheses, though any of the three would be grammatically correct. In "If that happens—heaven forbid—I don't know what I'll do," the dashes are used for emphasis.

- Indicates an unfinished thought or statement, much as ellipsis periods do, as in "He said, 'I'm telling you—' but never finished the sentence."

A.4.5 All About Apostrophes

Apostrophes are another punctuation mark that is often misused. Uses for apostrophes include:

- Turning a noun that does not end in "s" into a possessive noun, as in "the cat's bed" or "the book's cover."

- Used by itself at the end of a word, an apostrophe forms a possessive for a plural noun ending in "s," as in 'the nurses' lounge," "many stores' policies," and "the boys' camping trip."

- It is correct to either use an apostrophe by itself after an "s" or with an additional "s" to create a possessive for a singular noun that ends in "s." "Tiger Woods' wife should hate him" and "Tiger Woods's wife should hate him' are both correct. But "Tiger Wood's wife should hate him" is incorrect, since his last name is Woods, not Wood.

- Make an indefinite pronoun possessive, as in "one's convictions," someone's car," or "anyone's guess." But never use an apostrophe to make a definite pronoun possessive, since these words are already possessive (hers, yours, its, theirs).

- Do not use an apostrophe to make a noun except a letter of the alphabet or a number plural. Many people mistakenly write things like "The Smith's arrived five minutes ago" to pluralize the name. Do use an apostrophe, however, to pluralize "mind your p's and q's" or "the 1990's."
- Form a contraction where the apostrophe replaces missing letters or numbers, as in "wasn't" (a contraction for was not), "six o'clock" (a contraction for

on the clock), or "class of '84" (a contraction for class of 1984).

A.4.6 Quotation Marks

Few punctuation marks cause more confusion than quotation marks do. I've wrestled with whether or not to use them with many of the examples I've made up in this book, and many writers also have trouble deciding where quotation marks go in relation to other punctuation marks. Here are the basic rules:

- Quotation marks always come in pairs.

- Final quotation marks come after a comma, period, question mark or exclamation point. Examples: "Go home," she said. "How does it work?" he asked. He said, "I'm finished." But final quotation marks come before a colon or semicolon, as in Read Whitman's "Leaves of Grass"; it represents his finest work.

- Use double quotation marks to enclose a direct quote. Use single quotation marks to enclose a quote within a quote, as in "I heard him say, 'You're going to regret this' before he disappeared."

- If a direct quote lasts for more than one paragraph, use the begin quote marks at the beginning of each paragraph, but only use end quote marks after the last paragraph ends.
- Do not use quotation marks around thoughts, indirect quotes, or paraphrased sentences.

- Use quotes to indicate technical jargon, as in Policemen often refer to criminals as "perps" and Doctors often say a dying patient is "circling the drain."

- Use quotes to illustrate an example, as in "This is an example of an example."

- Use quotes around the titles of most poems, songs, articles, stories, or short musical compositions. Use italics or underline titles of books, magazines, newspapers, movies, plays, long poems, works of art, symphonies, and proper names of ships, airplanes, or spacecraft.

A.4.7 Exclamation Points

Writers tend to overuse exclamation points. Use them only to indicate a command, surprise, or very strong emotion, as in "Please help us!" "Forward march!" or "I'm amazed!" Using exclamation points freely dampens their impact. As F. Scott Fitzgerald wrote, "Cut out all those exclamation marks. An exclamation mark is like laughing at your own joke."

A.5 Unbreakable Rules

As you have no doubt gathered from reading this chapter, many rules of grammar and word usage are open to interpretation and can be broken on occasion. There are some rules, however, that are non-negotiable. Here are some no-no's that are NEVER acceptable in English usage (unless contained in a direct quote):
- ain't (isn't is correct)
- all the farther (drop "all the". Farther by itself is correct)
- anywheres (anywhere is correct)

- nowheres (nowhere is correct)
- somewheres (somewhere is correct)
- being as (being or being that are correct)
- can't hardly (can hardly is correct)
- double negatives, such as can't get no jobs
- could of (could have is correct)
- desire to (desire is correct)
- disregardless or irregardless (regardless is correct)
- had of (had is correct)
- in regards to (regarding is correct)
- inside of (inside is correct)
- outside of (outside is correct)
- might of (might have is correct)
- muchly (much is correct)
- should of (should have is correct)
- would of (would have is correct)
- phone up (phone is correct)
- pretend like (pretend that is correct)
- right good (very good is correct)
- this here (this is correct)
- where... at (instead of I don't know where she is at, use I don't know where she is)
- is comprised of (comprises is correct)

Good Grammar

Think of good grammar as your friend and as part of your ticket to writing success, rather than as a bunch of pain-in-the-neck rules. If you want to write well, you must use language, punctuation, and spelling correctly. No ifs, ands, or buts.

Appendix B
Referencing References

Most publishers adhere to *The Chicago Manual of Style* for citing references, but some request alternate methods. Be sure to check writer's guidelines for publisher preferences.

B.1 Citing Books

For a book reference, *The Chicago Manual of Style* requires listing the author's last name, comma, first name, comma, italicized book title, comma, publisher's place of business, colon, publisher's name, comma, and year of publication. A sample book citation looks like this: Smith, John, *The Roman Empire*, Columbus, OH: Garrett Publishing, 2009. If a book has more than one author, the names are separated by the word "and."

B.2 Citing Magazine Articles

For a magazine article citation, list the author's last name, comma, first name, comma, article title in quotes, comma, italicized publication name, comma, month and year of publication, comma, page numbers. A sample is Lange, Paul, "The Best of the Bunch," *Grapevine Quarterly*, September 2008, pp. 40-45.

Journal article citations differ slightly from those of magazine articles because they usually include a volume number. The proper citation is author's last name, comma, author's first name, comma, article title in quotes, comma, italicized journal name, no comma, volume number, month and year in parentheses, colon, page numbers. A sample is Davis, Ron, "A Double-

Blind Study of a Novel Monoclonal Antibody," *Journal of Cancer Research* 43 (December 2010): 172-185. It is acceptable, but not necessary, to write Vol. in front of the volume number, and if you add this, use a comma after the journal name. If pp. appears before the page number numerals, a comma instead of a colon is used. Some journals list issue numbers instead of or in addition to dates and volume numbers. This may be listed after the journal name, followed by a comma, as in *Journal of Cancer Research*, no. 18 (2010), pp. 172-185.

B.3 Citing Newspaper Articles

Newspaper citations are listed as title of the article in quotes, comma, newspaper name in italics, comma, date, comma, section number, if applicable, comma, and page number. "A New Perspective on Old Clothes," *New York Times*, January 3, 2010, sec. 5, p. H12.

B.4 Citing Web References

For Websites or online articles, the usual citation format is to list the Website or author name first, then the article title in quotes, and then the complete Web address. If the article appeared in a particular magazine or journal and is available online, this information can also be listed. Examples are

Centers For Disease Control, "Statistics on Accidental Poisonings," www.cdc.gov/statistics/poisonings.html.

Jones, Jane, "Following Your Nose," *ENT Proceedings*, June 2009, www.ent.org/Jun2009/Jones/follow.htm.

B.5 Citing Interviews

List all people you have interviewed, professional affiliations (if applicable), dates, and contact information in a bibliography as well.

B.6 Sample Bibliography

A sample bibliography might look like this:

Bibliography for "Animal Zzzzs"

Doe, Jane, *Animals Sleep*, New York: Rimon and Simon Publishers, 2008.

Wood, Sam, "The Neurology of Animal Sleep,:" *National Journal of Neurology*, Vol. 22, October 2010, pp. 201-207.

San Diego Zoo, "Mammals Asleep,"
www.sdzoo.org/animalbytes.pdf.

Francis, Caron, "Sleepy Snippets," *Science Weekly,* June 25, 2009, www.scienceweekly.com/article/sleepysnippets/jun252009.html
.

Author interview with Elmer Expert, Zoologist at the Smithsonian National Zoo, November 8, 2011, 555-555-5555, ee@snz.edu.

Author interview with Bobbie Biologist, Professor of Neurobiology at the University of California, Los Angles, November 10, 2011, 555-444-4444, bbneuro@ucla.edu.

About the Author

Melissa Abramovitz grew up in San Diego, California and graduated summa cum laude from the University of California, San Diego with a degree in psychology in 1976. She has always loved to write, and began writing professionally in 1986 to allow her to be a stay-at-home mom when her two children were small. Since then she has published hundreds of nonfiction magazine articles for children, teens, and adults. She has also published numerous short stories, poems, educational series books, and picture books for children and teenagers, as well as one adult novella. She currently lives in Roseville, California.

www.ingramcontent.com/pod-product-compliance
Lightning Source LLC
Chambersburg PA
CBHW080526090426
42733CB00015B/2506